SPECIAL EDUCATION SERIES
Peter Knoblock, *Editor*

Schooling Children with Down Syndrome

TOWARD AN UNDERSTANDING OF POSSIBILITY

Christopher Kliewer

FOREWORD BY DOUGLAS BIKLEN

Teachers College, Columbia University
New York and London

Published by Teachers College Press, 1234 Amsterdam Avenue, New York, NY 10027

Library of Congress Cataloging-in-Publication Data

Kliewer, Christopher.
   Schooling children with Down syndrome : toward an understanding of
possibility / Christopher Kliewer ; foreword by Douglas Biklen.
     p.   cm. — (Special education series)
   Includes bibliographical references and index.
   ISBN 0-8077-3731-3 (paper : alk. paper). — ISBN 0-8077-3732-1
(cloth : alk. paper)
    1. Mentally handicapped children—Education—Social aspects—
United States. 2. Down syndrome—Social aspects—United States.
3. Educational anthropology—United States. I. Title. II. Series:
Special education series (New York, N.Y.)
   LC4631.K55   1998
   371.92'8—dc21   97-47391

ISBN 0-8077-3731-3 (paper)
ISBN 0-8077-3732-1 (cloth)

Printed on acid-free paper
Manufactured in the United States of America

05 04 03 02 01 00 99 98   8 7 6 5 4 3 2 1

For my dad, Ken, who never hesitates
to tell me, "Think, kid."
And for my mom, Kathy, who's sure to
let me know that I do.

Contents

Foreword

A number of years ago I came across a quotation on a pamphlet published by a self-advocacy group in Melbourne, Australia, that read, "Don't think that we don't think." It struck me as both ironic and resistive, since the statement came from people who had been labeled intellectually disabled (in Melbourne at the time, the term *mentally retarded* was out of vogue, deemed too prejudicial). What did the slogan mean, exactly? That people labeled intellectually disabled do think, even if not at the "level" of other people? Did it mean to say, "Don't presume to know *what* we think?" Or was it a more robust claim: "We think just fine, so take us seriously."

To me, it could easily have meant any of the above, but at least it meant, "Don't ever assume that the label of intellectual disability (or mental retardation) justifies banishment of a whole group of people. It resonated for me, perhaps because it fit with so many of my experiences over the years in the fields of special education, disability rights, deinstitutionalization/ community integration, and inclusive education. It reminded me of the time that a man labeled retarded, who had been institutionalized for more than 6 years in a mental retardation facility, asked me the meaning of the word *dearth*, saying "*Dearth*. Does that mean little?" I wondered how it was that a retarded person could even ask the question. It made me recall people with cerebral palsy who once were thought retarded and then, upon finding a means of communication, emerged as best-selling authors (e.g., C. Brown, 1989; Nolan, 1987; and McDonald [Crossley & McDonald, 1984]). It made me think of an elementary-age student with Down syndrome who supposedly was retarded but could read as well as his nondisabled peers. And it reminded me of a student with Rett syndrome who had been presumed by a school psychologist to be severely retarded. Her mother had been told that since tests showed that she could not reach a bell and make it ring, or any number of other physical tasks, she was not intelligent. But this mother saw something different. Always expectant of her daughter's competence, the mother saw her rap on the table that held the psychologist's bell, making it ring. Her mother concluded, "She not only understood the request, she concocted her own modification of the test to make a correct answer." Besides, her father explained, "She laughs and smiles at jokes, and shakes her head, slightly, to say no." In the ninth grade, she made the honor roll for the first time in her years of schooling.

At its core, the "Don't think we don't think" statement poses two fundamental questions for the fields of disability and education, and for society at large, two questions that are central to Christopher Kliewer's book, SCHOOLING CHILDREN WITH DOWN SYNDROME. They are: (1) How do you know what someone knows? (2) What are the consequences of presuming incompetence?

For the person who has difficulties in speaking and acting—which includes many individuals with Down syndrome—knowing what someone knows requires an inquiring teacher, parent, friend, or other to seek intimacy. Any person desiring to know what and how another thinks must be willing to adopt a position of radical openness, seeking more to inquire than to judge (Bogdan & Taylor, 1976; Crossley & McDonald, 1984; Moon, 1992; Oppenheim, 1977).

In many people's minds, Down syndrome is the quintessential icon of mental retardation. Although the idea of mental retardation may have begun as a metaphor—seeing the person who responds slowly or not at all, someone must have declared, "It's as if the mind is retarded"—it now has become thought of as real, embodied in particular people, physically observable. Yet in this book, Kliewer thoroughly, with the most carefully drawn evidence, dismantles the prevailing presumption of deficit in anyone so labeled. In wonderfully unrelenting terms, to examine how Down syndrome is constructed, Kliewer asks what it means in the culture, in schools, in families, and to people who "have it." Setting the context for what Down syndrome comes to mean in schools, Kliewer describes the racist origins of the term *mongolism* and its place in eugenicists' thoughts; he shows us how such ideas have driven what has been "known" about Down syndrome. But more importantly, he uncovers a century-long cover-up of competence—for years individual people with Down syndrome have shown normal competence in reading and thought yet have consistently had their abilities ignored, even denied. It is disturbing to find that so much of this cover-up was conducted by leading scholars, usually in the name of caring and always using the language and authority of "disability science," where equality and justice are appropriated for professional practice to adjudicate.

Through Kliewer's observation of students with Down syndrome in public school classes, most often with their nondisabled peers, we come to see how context shapes understandings (recognitions and denials) of competence. Painfully, in some instances, we see obvious evidence of ability either missed or explained away, even *in* classrooms where students with Down syndrome attend with nondisabled students. Reassuringly, we also see scenes of students with Down syndrome engaging in intellectual work in schools, also in typical classrooms with nondisabled students, and being appreciated and supported for their contributions. In these latter situations, radical openness allows teachers to transcend the boundaries of the dominant deficit ideology that frames Down syndrome as retardation.

Although they never asked to be so, teachers are society's principal surrogates for constructing what Down syndrome means. Predictably, their attitudes exist on a continuum of understandings about ability/disability, with one end of the range presuming incompetence and the other competence. In their practice and their negotiation with particular students can be found the implications of adopting one or the other presumption. Presuming incompetence allows educators to dismiss students' learning, to overlook abilities and contributions, and to see nothing but failure. In contrast, presuming competence allows the educator to see the other person as a peer; it requires a democratic outlook, a commitment to justice. The presumption of competence allows education to being. What's remarkable here is not that such work has begun but that it is as extensive, rich, and complex as it is.

Kliewer asks the same question that serious educators should always ask: What are the situations or conditions in which students seem to break through? This question has a special meaning for students with disabilities, given that they must break through their own difficulties with performance—disability can get in the way of saying and doing what the person may intend—as well as deficit ideologies. Perhaps because of the dominant stereotype that frames any success of a person with a disability as the product of unbelievable courage and personal heroics, this question is too infrequently asked.

Sometimes, of course, teachers create situations in which they may not know exactly who learns, or how and what they learn. This book evoked in me recollection of one such situation. I was just finishing an hour-long lecture on research related to communication by people with severe disabilities, including cerebral palsy and autism. The lecture concerned how many individuals with such impairments were typically thought to be mentally retarded prior to discovering an effective means of communication. Recent research was causing me and other researchers as well as many educators and parents to rethink how mental retardation is constructed. The research suggested a seemingly obvious question: Is it fair to judge mental retardation on the basis of what someone can say or do? Do tests based on students having speech and pointing skills (e.g., intelligence tests) really tell us what a person who lacks these abilities may be thinking or the degree to which someone is able to think?

When I had nearly finished the lecture—I was just beginning my conclusion—a young woman with Down syndrome got up from her front-row seat and approached the podium, holding out a piece of paper with writing on it. I looked at the writing but was unable to read it; it appeared to be scrawls intended to look like writing, but not real words. Her speech was limited to one- and two-word utterances, and I simply could not understand what she seemed so intent on telling me. I thanked her for showing me her writing, invited her to wait a few minutes for me to finish, and then spoke with her later, explaining as best I could that I sensed she was interested in what I had been saying. Later I learned that some of her care workers were beginning to introduce her to typing and had found that she could communicate in sentences when typing. About a year later this same woman participated in a research project in which she demonstrated that she could not only communicate in sentences but could also play computer games involving adult-level literacy skills.

I recalled quite vividly how this woman had interrupted me momentarily at my public lecture. And I remembered thinking at the time that she might want to develop literacy skills similar to those I described. What I did not know at the time and probably could not have known was that this woman was *already* literate but simply had no way of telling the world. Her handing me the paper with writing that looked like words was probably a gesture to indicate that. Later, with the aide of a computer keyboard, she was able to reveal her literary skills. The lesson for me was that it's often hard to know exactly how students engage with particular learning opportunities and that there is no rational reason to presume a lack of engagement simply because the person does not have an effective means of communication or because a person's actions are not understood with any certainty (e.g., producing unintelligible scrawls). Not being able to say something is not the same as not having something to say.

This book is peppered with example after example, in several schools, of how teachers can create situations in which the student with Down syndrome can move from being an exile or tolerated immigrant in relation to mainstream education to being an active participant, with nondisabled peers, in democratic classroom life. We see two preschool students, one with Down syndrome, whose friendship derives from their shared love of books and literacy. We see a teacher who learns that abrupt, seemingly intrusive noises and blundering movements by a student may be attempts to get correct words out or to make a point through gesture, rather than disruptive acts. Kliewer explains that this teacher "listens deeply to the sounds of competence" in a student. Possessing what I have called "radical openness," the teacher knows to pay attention to any bit of evidence that a student thinks in complex ways, realizing that no amount of failed performances can erase any single instance of competent speech or action.

We see another student with Down syndrome who nearly disrupts his inclusive class when he becomes bored at the slow pace of work expected from him and his classmates; his astute teacher senses the cause of his behavior and picks up the pace. As I read such passages and admired how Kliewer links them nearly seamlessly with the theoretical frameworks of Dewey, Vygotsky, Gardner, Ashton-Warner, and others, I could not help wondering if readers will understand the importance of this work. It links how we think about education in general with how we *must* think about education for students with Down syndrome and other disabilities. Nothing in this work, save perhaps the specific details of examples, differs from thousands of other educational situations that occur daily, involving so-called nondisabled students. This book, by taking Down syndrome as its focus, lets the educational choices and challenges related to inclusive schooling serve as a metaphor for all education. Through each of many classroom and other situations, Kliewer shows us how knowing what someone knows is always mediated by context and viewer. His observations reveal the rich details of exemplary teaching practice, suggesting specific ideas about how teachers can elicit effective student participation in the academic and social life of classrooms. His analysis frames a democratic theory of inclusion, whereby those who presume competence often seem to encounter it—and allows us to adjust our own understandings of Down syndrome from deficit to promise, and of education from exclusion to community.

Douglas Biklen
Syracuse University

Preface

In 1992 I began a study on the cultural meaning of Down syndrome in the school lives of children. My interest was not in the mass of psychological and medical manuscripts that constitute so much of our educational understanding of students with disabilities. Rather, I wanted to learn about disability from the inside, by joining children with Down syndrome in their everyday relationships with friends, peers, teachers, and others who make up the school community.

Over the course of two school years, I followed 10 children with Down syndrome, aged 3 to 10, across 13 classrooms. I diligently recorded the stories of their daily experiences, spent extensive time with their teachers, and managed numerous free meals as I was invited into the children's homes to learn from their families. I have combined the stories I systematically gathered in the tradition of ethnographic research with accounts of high school–aged students in order to provide a detailed picture of schooling, Down syndrome, and disability.

Ethnography has grown in stature as an educational research approach for ascertaining social understanding. In this method, termed *qualitative research*, meaning and understanding is found not necessarily in laboratories, random samples, co-variants, or control groups but in themes and stories that emerge from a deep understanding of the contexts and situations of everyday life (Bogdan & Biklen, 1992).

On entering classrooms in which the meaning of Down syndrome was constructed in the relationships among students, teachers, and materials, I encountered children struggling with cultural perceptions as to their community value, capacities, potential, and worth. They existed, in a sense, as *nonconformists*, often separated from what it means to be a *good student*. Documenting this struggle led me to examine literature and research that helped me better understand what it means to be a nonconformist student in school: a societal institution that, in large part, measures students' worth by the degree of their conformity to established patterns of behavior (Gardner, 1983).

The struggles I witnessed in schools, combined with literature that tells the story of groups of people transforming the very meaning of community value (e.g., Ashton-Warner, 1963; D. Biklen, 1992; Dyson, 1993, Kozol, 1991), provides us with a mosaic of contrasting school cultures and contradictory representations of Down syndrome, disability, and human difference. Only by tracing these representations to their underlying assumptions can we come to understand the competing moralities according to which a student's value and humanness are either acknowledged or questioned. Ultimately, this book is an effort to expose these moral foundations and to describe an educational framework that finds community value in each of our unique ways of being human.

OUTLINE OF THE BOOK

Chapter 1 provides an overview of the contrasting cultural images of individuals with Down syndrome, the moral frameworks from which these representations stem, and the way they translate into current educational practices. The prevailing societal perception of people with Down syndrome as community burdens relegates students with Down syndrome to what I term the school status of the alien or squatter. In contrast to this framework of cultural devaluation, a competing understanding of disability and difference conceptualizes students with Down syndrome as inherently valuable members of the community. This interpretation of difference creates opportunities for what I call classroom citizenship. Included in this chapter is a brief description of my own journey from viewing particular people as inherently burdensome to realizing their community potential, value, dignity, and inherent self-worth.

Chapter 2 outlines the history of community banishment of people with disabilities that has resulted in their status as alien and squatter. This history exposes the distinctly nonscientific origins of the current practice of segregating children with disabilities—a practice often claimed to be a matter of disability science. Within this historical analysis, I document the delineation of Down syndrome as a category of the *less-than-human*, and follow contrasting patterns of treatment to today's image of the individual who is inherently burdensome to schools.

Chapter 3 depicts current school segregation of students with Down syndrome encountered in my study and uncovers a commutative law positioning Down syndrome as a primary societal image of mental retardation. I describe the assumptions behind the commutative law of Down syndrome used to support the status of the alien and squatter—and then dismantle this segregationist logic. In doing so, the label "mental retardation" is exposed as a metaphor that has come to represent the appearance, performances, and mannerisms of students with Down syndrome.

Chapter 4 describes classrooms that resist the cultural devaluation of students with Down syndrome. I present images of students, teachers, and families as participants in the restructuring of schools to support diverse learners. Rather than experiencing segregation, children who do not fit the traditional image of *the good student* are recognized as uniquely valuable to the web of relationships that form the classroom community. I analyze the assumptions on which one's classroom citizenship is ascribed and argue, based on observation, that valued community connections are fundamental to realizing any student's individual developmental capacities.

In Chapter 5, I describe how establishing valued community connections leads students with Down syndrome toward citizenship in classroom *literate communities*. This is a fundamentally valuable school location for children if they are to be considered *good students*, and one that traditionally has been closed to students with Down syndrome. Their appearance and performance separated them from what it meant to be a reader and writer in school. The reconfiguration of literacy from an end-product of a rigid curriculum to a dynamic language-based form of expression is documented.

Chapter 6 describes how establishing valued community connections leads to a reinterpretation of *problem behaviors* associated with Down syndrome and disability. Each child's behavior is described as a way for that child to make sense of the classroom culture as he or she experiences it. Citizenship, in turn, opens possibilities for the formation of mutually valuing relationships and, ultimately, the construction of friendships.

In the conclusion, I draw together the themes presented throughout the book in a synthesized discussion of the meaning of citizenship in the school lives of students with Down syndrome. I revisit the moral framework that posits community connection as the foundation on which one's humanness is constructed and present a representation of students with Down syndrome as inherently valuable to the classroom community. I end with a call for the elimination of segregated schooling.

Acknowledgments

Particular data presented in Chapter 5 appeared initially in *Exceptional Children*, in my article "Citizenship in the Literate Community: An Ethnography of Children with Down syndrome and the Written Word." I appreciate the editors' permission to include this data.

I owe a tremendous thanks to the students, teachers, and families who participated in my original study. Their experiences, in essence, authored this book.

I also wish to thank my colleague Kathie East for her thoughtful criticisms of early drafts of this book. She offered much insight.

The book would not have been written were it not for the lengthy discussions I engaged in with Sandra Alper, Deb Gallagher, Carmen Montecinos, and John Smith, all at the University of Northern Iowa. Though each, I am sure, would like me to make clear I am fully responsible for ideas presented, their support in all aspects of my life has been invaluable. I also appreciate the ever-present support provided by the entire Department of Special Education at the University of Northern Iowa.

I am indebted to my teachers at Syracuse University for their time and commitment to my research development. I would especially like to acknowledge Bob Bogdan's, Peter Knoblock's, and Steve Taylor's influence on my thinking.

I owe a special thanks to Doug Biklen at Syracuse University. He is, and will always remain, my teacher.

Thanks, also, to Zan, a magical teacher, and Kellan, an inspiration. And finally, I appreciate the support Angie continuously provides me in the drama of life.

Schooling Children with Down Syndrome

1

The Struggle for Citizenship: Schools and the Representation of Down Syndrome

I opened the newspaper one morning in 1995 to a story about a woman with Down syndrome named Sandra Jensen, who lived and, it appeared, would soon die in Sacramento, California. Because of chronic respiratory distress resulting in progressive difficulty in circulating blood to her lungs, she required a heart–lung transplant in order to survive beyond 1 year. She was, however, refused the necessary medical procedure at the University of California at San Diego Hospital and the Stanford University Medical Center (Bronston, 1995).

Doctors and hospital spokespersons justified the refusal by explaining that Sandra was an "inappropriate" organ recipient. The reason: Because of her "serious mental retardation," Sandra, it was thought, would be incapable of caring for herself during recovery following the operation (Goldberg, 1996). Care included taking an array of medications and exercising regularly. Never mind that Sandra had supported herself busing tables, had held a multitude of volunteer positions including terms served as president of the local Capital People First disability rights organization, had maintained her own apartment with minimal personal assistance, and had lived quite well in her Sacramento neighborhood.

The presence of a trisomy of her 21st chromosome, the genetic etiology of Down syndrome, effectively positioned Sandra, for a time, at the periphery of medicine. Doctors considered her a socially and culturally expendable human being: a community burden not worth the precious medical resources available to save her life.

Over the course of several months, I continued reading about Sandra Jensen in the news. The medical decision to reject Sandra's organ candidacy resulted in a public outcry reminiscent of a somewhat similar situation in Indiana in 1982. In this case, the parents of Baby Doe, born with Down syndrome and an easily repairable esophagus obstruction, elected with the support of doctors to starve the infant to death. The Indiana Supreme Court ruled Baby Doe's infanticide legal.

The court's decision resulted in a widespread social uproar uniting the political left and right in an effort to save the child through medical treatment and adoption. However, the wheels of appellate justice moved slowly, and a baby's stamina in the face of starvation is limited. While the movement to save Baby Doe's life failed, the struggle to save Sandra Jensen's succeeded: Stanford reversed its decision, and doctors performed the heart-lung procedure in January of 1996. Sandra diligently followed the recovery schedule and became an eloquent national spokesperson for the societal value of all people with disabilities and their civil right to full citizenship.

The drugs Sandra required to suppress her immune system in order that her body not reject the new organs eventually took their toll on her health—as they do to so many individuals who undergo similar extreme medical efforts. Sandra eventually developed lymphoma, a common side effect, and in May of 1997 she lapsed into a coma from which she did not recover (Wilson, 1997). Her cardiologist noted, "This was a complication that can occur with anyone who has a transplant. I want to emphasize that it had nothing to do with her as a person, or as someone with Down syndrome" (quoted in Hubert, 1997, p. A1).

THE CONTRADICTORY REPRESENTATIONS OF DOWN SYNDROME

The struggles of Sandra Jensen and Baby Doe reflect a tumultuous paradox in the social meaning of Down syndrome at the edge of a new millennium. Contradictory representations, each rooted in the convoluted discourses of history, position people with Down syndrome and, by extension, all people with disabilities at contesting cultural locations of competence, potential, and worth. Certain of these representations suggest that resources be provided to individuals with Down syndrome that maintain their stigma and low social status: Deny Sandra the appropriate medical treatment necessary for continued community involvement, but pour vast amounts of resources into the welfare and custodial care she will require while we wait for her to die. Other representations, however, acknowledge Sandra's human worth and her right to resources that will maintain and enhance her connection to the wider community.

The Representation of Burden

As it now stands, the dominant societal representation of Down syndrome against which Sandra Jensen and Baby Doe struggled is grounded in social traditions that attach a reduced value to particular differences associated with human variation and nonconformity. These *differences that matter*, the ones that constrict a nonconformist's social worth, are largely derived from *utilitarian individualism* (Soltis, 1993), a particular moral framework advanced in a consumer-driven democracy that values human relationships only as they relate to individuals striving to accrue cultural power, wealth, and privilege (MacPherson, 1974).

Within the framework of utilitarian individualism, *social good* (i.e., "the common good") is thought to derive solely from one's individual utility, intrinsic ability, and personal performance, with society being enriched when individuals attain their personal ends (Bellah, Madsen, Sullivan, Swidler, & Tipton, 1985). Those who are perceived as contributing (or who are considered to have the potential to contribute) to society's economic and cultural goals are given the rights of citizenship, while those considered to lack individual (hence, social) utility are subjected to varying degrees of what is thought to be a natural and necessary segregation from community opportunities. The logic underlying this particular vision of *democracy* suggests, of course, that the greatest good for the greatest number will come from diverting finite opportunities to the few who can and will actually turn them into increased wealth, power, and opportunities.

Embedded within these assumptions of stratified worth, Down syndrome represents one category of the *differences that matter*. Human variations associated with Down syndrome form what is commonly considered a *condition* of global defect naturally resulting in an individual who is an economic and social burden to the community. The label of "burden," once applied, carries with it connotations of a cultural black hole sucking in the precious resources of the community while emitting nothing of value in return, thereby leaving less for those of us who might individually advance the common good. Thus, on utilitarian grounds, Baby Doe and, initially, Sandra Jensen were denied opportunities available to those of us who do not embody the differences that matter.

The reversal of the hospital decision to effectively end Sandra Jensen's life, made under intense pressure from Sandra and her allies, points out that the status of community burden is neither a singular nor essential consequence of Down syndrome. Rather, distinguishing people with Down syndrome as *inherently* expendable exists within a larger set of representations as just one discourse of disability: one particular moral stance that relegates people with certain differences to the cultural periphery of a community, leaving central space for those of us who conform to the utilitarian standard of a contributing citizen.

Throughout history, people with Down syndrome and other disabilities have shared the cultural periphery of hopelessness with others who have been construed as community burdens—as individuals with differences that matter. In twentieth-century America alone, the list of social outcasts is nearly endless. At one point or another (and several consistently), women (generally), blacks, Catholics, Slavs, Chicanos, single mothers (specifically), Latinos, Italians, the Irish, the old, the poor, veterans (no less!), working mothers (again specifically), Jews, orphans, and Asians have all been represented as societal burdens and have been subjected to some form of community segregation and reduced opportunity. (And this is just a partial list!)

The Representation of Community Value

I noted with interest and wrote a letter of congratulations when the newspaper reported that Sandra Jensen and her allies had successfully pressured Stanford doctors to perform the life-saving operation. The reversal was, of course, a great victory for Sandra personally. It also reflected a battle won in the wider struggle engaged in by people with disabilities and their supporters to smash the image of burden attached to human variation and build in its place a representation of hope, potential, dignity, and value.

This struggle by and for people with disabilities rejects the cultural *utility* of segregation, whether it takes an environmental, intellectual, spiritual, or lethal form. Segregation (ironically) diverts tremendous amounts of resources toward structuring an existential location of hopelessness entrapping people whose very humanness is in question. For instance, a current, common practice is to place individuals with disabilities in nursing homes regardless of their age. Children, youths, young adults, and those who have reached middle age are increasingly finding themselves in long-term-care facilities originally designed to efficiently remove older Americans from the community. The cost of this practice is enormous, often exceeding $100,000 per individual per year (Shapiro, 1994, p. 240).

In resistance to a history of segregation (see Chapter 2), an advocacy movement has emerged that seeks to change the meaning of disability to one of community membership—in essence, full citizenship. The movement is grounded in principles of social justice formed in the realization of human reciprocity: a moral position collectively recognizing that we each, as human beings, possess a unique value that adds to and strengthens the cultural fabric of society (D. Biklen, 1992, 1993; Bogdan & Taylor, 1989; Knoblock, 1982). To be valued as fully human is to share in democratic citizenship: family citizenship (Kingsley & Levitz, 1994), school citizenship (Grandin & Scariano, 1986), community citizenship (Snow, 1988), and cultural citizenship (Andrews, 1995). It means an end to segregation that reduces certain of us who share in the differences that matter to a status of less-than-human (Bogdan & Taylor, 1994).

The realization of human reciprocity, as the phrase suggests, cannot occur in isolation. Our humanness (or our construed lack thereof) emerges in the relationships we form with other members of the human family. To be considered fully human requires acceptance into relationships in which the experiences that form our individuality are recognized as communally valuable. The experiences we each bring to the cultural table add to the many courses of community even as we are nourished by the experiences of others. In this sense, reciprocity is democratic communication as delineated by the twentieth-century educator John Dewey (1916). He recognized human association and dialogue as central to building a just community: Each of our voices, no matter how indecipherable it may sound, strengthens the ever-evolving web of relationships from which a democratic community is formed. The oppressive silencing of even one voice through any form of segregation eliminates that set of experiences from our collective conversation and diminishes the culture of the community.

UTILITARIANISM VERSUS HUMAN RECIPROCITY IN THE REPRESENTATION OF DISABILITY

In the 1940s, Leo Kanner (perhaps best known for his early description of autism) sought to articulate a version of the principle of human reciprocity. His effort (Kanner, 1942) was in response to an article by Foster Kennedy (1942) in which Kennedy argued from a utilitarian point of view that people with what were then considered moderate and severe disabilities should be killed:

> The idiot and the imbecile seem to me unresponsive to the care put upon them. They are not capable of being educated; nor can such defective products ever be made to be so. Good breeding begets good brains; with no good brains there can be no good mind. (p. 13)

Kennedy felt that the "high-grade morons" should be allowed to live in institutionalized settings but was "in favor of euthanasia for those hopeless ones who should never have been born—Nature's mistakes" (p. 14).

Kanner (1942) responded to Kennedy that throughout history "man's need for self-assurance has always prompted him to look down with contempt or contemptuous pity on those whose disadvantages or misfortunes he did not happen to share" (p. 17). Kanner noted that Western culture has traditionally attached community value to perceptions of intellectual performance but argued that "mind" (our social presence) and tested intelligence have little to do with one another. He contrasted his garbage collector's assistant, who was considered to have a low IQ but was thoughtful and caring, to a young man whose tested intelligence had "hit the ceiling" but who demonstrated extreme selfishness: "We, the intellectual Haves, instinctively sense greater kinship with the unstable young blade, another Have, than with the garbage collector's assistant, an intellectual Have-not" (p. 18).

Kanner suggested that arbitrary divisions into haves and have-nots by the professions of psychiatry and psychology resulted in society's devaluation and elimination of the have-nots. His opposition to elimination emerged from a moral position that affirmed individual value in our shared humanity. To hold a different position, he suggested, would be the worst form of fascism:

> Shall we . . . take our cue from the Nazi Gestapo? Does anyone really think that the German nation is in any way improved, ennobled, made more civilized by inflicting what they cynically choose to call mercy deaths on the feebleminded? (Kanner, 1942, p. 21)

In a commentary on the contrasting positions of Kennedy and Kanner, the American Psychiatric Association (APA; 1942) decidedly rejected Kanner's suggestion that the community is a more valuable place when all are afforded citizenship:

> Dr. Kennedy favors [euthanasia] under legal sanction in certain carefully defined cases, and he offers strong arguments in support of his position. Dr. Kanner opposes this position but in his paper presents no arguments beyond the statement: "An idiotic child may have fond parents who want him alive." (p. 143)

The APA misrepresented Kanner's arguments of social reciprocity while disguising its own moral base within a rhetoric of the natural sciences:

> Scientists presumably have reached their conviction by more or less impersonal routes; the layman on the contrary who has the misfortune to be the parent of a low-grade defective is actuated by strongly personal motives which he may or may not be capable of setting out clearly in his own consciousness. (p. 143)

By hiding its morality in the jargon of objectivity, the APA positioned "clinically perfumed homicide" (Perske, 1987, p. 276) as a matter of science, not a human value position in which choices are made that deny the human-ness of particular people.

More than 50 years later, and 1 year after Sandra Jensen fought for the right to live, Bérubé returned to the debate between utilitarianism and social reciprocity in his insightful book on raising a child with Down syndrome. He dismissed the still-dominant moral position that located his young son, Jamie, to a status of reduced value because of his Down syndrome and argued that the *ideal* of community membership for all should emerge from a conversation in which we each add our voices to decisions on the meaning of human value. Bérubé (1996) noted:

> We would do well to seek the ground for human justice in our capacity to communicate with one another, regardless of whether we are incapable of uttering proper names, regardless of whether we mumble, regardless of whether we communicate by ASL. (p. 244)

In a democracy established on social reciprocity, Jamie Bérubé, Sandra Jensen, Baby Doe, and others who have Down syndrome would not be deterministically silenced. Nor could they be segregated from opportunities open to nondisabled citizens. Their community membership would be seen as essential to the evolving completeness of society as a whole: They are not burdens, they are not broken; they are representatives of the diversity of the human family (Kunc, 1993).

THE REPRESENTATION OF DOWN SYNDROME IN SCHOOL

Though arising in every social realm from medicine to welfare, the struggle over representation and its consequential treatment for people with Down syndrome may be most overt, and most heated, in the cultural endeavor of schooling. The specific purpose of this book is to describe the contesting meanings attached to Down syndrome in schools and to expose the historical and cultural assumptions from which they emerge. From this analysis, I present a framework for positioning the meaning of Down syndrome, disability, and difference at a location of value in which the right to citizenship in classroom communities and, by extension, in the wider community is extended to all people.

A Question of Membership: Translating Democracy to Schools

The conflict over the meaning of Down syndrome in schools is ultimately a question of community membership: Which students should have access to the regular routines, normal contexts, and general opportunities of the neighborhood schools, and which students can justifiably be denied school citizenship (and, by extension, community citizenship)? I was confronted with the conflicting responses to this question in a brief conversation during a morning visit to the East Ridge Early Childhood Center, a suburban, county-run preschool program outside a large East Coast city. East Ridge served as one of several research sites for my study of the cultural meaning of Down syndrome in school.

On this particular morning, I stood to the side watching a group of 4-year-old children dance, bounce, hop, and skip around a room called the "Race Space," a name reflective of the level and speed of movement encouraged by the mats, balls, trikes, and other equipment available for the children's use. On an earlier visit, I had learned that until the previous year, the Race Space was called the "Gross Motor Room." It had been used solely by East Ridge physical therapists as a location for developing the motor control of students with disabilities.

The name of the room was changed to the Race Space when the school itself was reorganized from a segregated special education program to a preschool that served children with and without disabilities in the same classrooms. Teachers noticed that the children without disabilities used the term *gross* as would be expected: "Like, 'you're gross, man,'" one teacher explained, "so we couldn't really be having therapy down in the 'gross' room!"

As I stood in the Race Space thinking about this shift in terminology, Mavis Sherrill approached me. Mavis was an East Ridge receptionist who also substituted for absent teachers. She was aware of my interest in students with Down syndrome, two of whom were members of the class I was observing.

Mavis and I chatted briefly about the progress of my study. Pointing toward Vic Schroeder, one of the students with Down syndrome, she said, "I have a neighbor friend with a grandson who has some speech thing, like a mild problem pronouncing some sounds. He was supposed to come here, but she was real upset. So was the mother. They really didn't agree he belonged with mongoloids—mongoloid children. He's going to private speech therapy now. He's doing real well." Ms. Sherrill shook her head and added, "You don't know, they might be right," referring to the decision to keep her neighbor's grandchild away from Vic and his classmate, Greg Lafrey, who also has Down syndrome.

I was stunned on hearing the expression *mongoloid* in reference to a student at East Ridge. Not that I wasn't familiar with the term, rooted in Dr. J. Langdon Down's original 1866 classification scheme in which he reorganized the general categories of congenital idiocy into specific subgroups related to a perceived intellectual and social hierarchy of ethnic categories. I understood that the racism of Dr. Down's age had remained an integral part of understanding Down syndrome well into the 1980s. I had even found myself telling people who appeared confused when asking about my research topic that, until fairly recently, Down syndrome was more commonly referred to as mongoloidism (or some such variation of the word *Mongol*). The confused expression was invariably replaced by a knowing smile: "Ah yes, mongoloid! I know them well."

The shock I felt at Mavis Sherrill's statement had only a little to do with the term *mongoloid* itself, as offensive as I found it. I realized Ms. Sherrill probably had little knowledge of the history of the label. Rather, I was taken aback by the impact of its connotations as they smashed the context of community I thought I was observing in the unrehearsed dance of childhood taking place in the Race Space. Here, with a teacher's help, Vic held the plastic handle of a toy gas pump, pretending to fill the imagined tanks of passing trikes steered by screaming children. Here Greg turned his three-wheeler head on into a classmate's vehicle, causing both boys to roll to the floor laughing with delight and bringing a stern warning from a passing teacher.

Yet within this hectic preschool togetherness, the paradox of Down syndrome emerged. East Ridge was a school in transition where children with disabilities were no longer segregated from their nondisabled peers. Vic and Greg had access to nonsecluded contexts that just the previous year would have been off limits. At the same time, the two preschoolers continued to serve particular people as symbols of the need for separation; they were identified as representatives of a category of personhood that required containment in educational locations apart from nondisabled children in a belief that the good of both groups would be served.

Social Utility and Schooling. The logic that would have Vic and Greg banished from opportunities to learn with nondisabled children is constructed on narrow and rigid interpretations of who and what constitutes community usefulness. Based on their representation as cultural burdens, students with Down syndrome and other disabilities have suffered a long history of segregation from the wider school community.

Utilitarianism translates into educational practices through the mediating social metatheory of functionalism. As Skrtic (1995b) has outlined, functionalism serves as the foundation of the modern social professions, including education and special education. It presupposes that the social world exists as an objective set of processes that are orderly in nature and inherently rational. Each element of the social world, then, including students (generally), teachers, and schools, has an objectively derived utility serving the mechanistic functioning of society. Special education, interestingly, functions (in conjunction with nursing homes and prisons) as a location for the removal of those particular students defined as nonfunctional burdens.

Human Reciprocity and Schooling. The principle of social justice based on human reciprocity rejects the functionalist definition of people with disabilities as self-evident obstacles to the smooth-running machinery of society. The struggle for community membership views segregation of people with disabilities as an act diminishing society as a whole in its banishment of particular sets of experiences from the relationships that make up a community's richness.

In the framework of human reciprocity, *impairment* constitutes a subjectively defined condition that results in the image of a burden *only when we choose to make it that*. The idea of defect is a social meaning, imposed on a particular set of experiences by people of higher status, that construes the individual or group in question as humanly deficient.

Reciprocity translates into educational practices through the mediating frameworks of various social constructivist and reconstructivist orientations toward schooling (Jungck & Marshall, 1992; Shannon, 1990; Weiler, 1988). Educational constructivism holds that social meaning is enacted on the world through the multiple understandings children build in relationships with others who share the classroom context. Functionalism suggests that an objective mold of citizenship preexists into which children must grow and fit if they are to become full members of the community. In contrast, constructivism recognizes that children cast and recast their own unique interpretations of the meaning of citizenship.

Reconstructivist orientations agree that knowledge and meaning are built by children through active engagement with one another, teachers, and materials, but they emphasize how such meaning might transform the wider community in the direction of valued membership for all. Though of distinct and contrasting philosophical origins, constructivism and reconstructivism share in a resistance to the notions that society generally and schools specifically are necessarily rational and orderly, and that certain individuals and groups of students are objectively and inherently burdensome to the school community.

Those who support the idea of citizenship for all students seek not to label and segregate particular people as defective; rather, they find value in their experiences and recognize that their educational participation is necessary for schooling to be complete (D. Biklen, 1985). In so doing, cultural stratification is transformed into supportive relationships as individuals and groups that embody the differences that matter are reconceptualized as full citizens of the family, classroom, neighborhood, and community.

The contesting images of burden versus valued human being that were attached to Vic and Greg in preschool will likely remain a site of struggle affecting their education throughout their schooling. For instance, in 1995 Dawn Recker, a young woman with Down syndrome in Iowa who was a high school graduate, sought admittance into a local community college. Her application was denied by administrators who defined her as "[unable] to demonstrate the ability to benefit from the educational programming for which [Dawn] is applying" (quoted in Ballard, 1995, p. A7). One administration official explained, "We're sitting here with an enrollment that's doubled in three years. Where do we find the space?" At a neighboring university, an art history professor found *the space*: At his invitation, Dawn sat in on a history course, and she has continued to attend classes at the university with a focus on early childhood education.

School Representations: The Alien, the Squatter, and the Citizen

The paradox in meaning I experienced at the East Ridge School and Dawn's battle to attend college reflect the contradictory interpretations of Down syndrome that emerged from the observations and experiences recorded in my study on the cultural representation of Down syndrome in schools. From my research, three broad school representations of Down syndrome became apparent: the alien, the squatter, and the citizen. Each image placed students with Down syndrome in different cultural locations of value in relation to the wider school community.

The Alien. The image of the alien, reflective of utilitarian and functional assumptions of disability as a community burden, presumes that students with Down syndrome are intellectually and developmentally defective. This underlying defectiveness is thought to result in educational needs considered foreign and burdensome to the teaching methods of regular education and the learning needs of nondisabled students. The children with Down syndrome are educationally segregated from their nondisabled peers, with only brief forays into the wider school community. The alien represents community membership overtly denied.

The Squatter. The image of the squatter maintains the utilitarian and functionalist view of students with Down syndrome as community burdens with reduced educational potential. However, space is made available for their learning needs at the periphery of the regular classroom community.

The squatter's inclusion is based on the assumption that all people have a democratic right to participate in the community. But this inclusion effectively creates a new border within the regular classroom, with one (minority) side containing *the defective* and their specialized learning needs and the other (majority) side containing *the nondefective* and their general educational needs. The squatter represents the struggle for citizenship stalled at the margins of the classroom community.

The Citizen. The image of the citizen represents persons with disabilities not as social burdens but as valued human beings. Students with Down syndrome are not educationally segregated based on presumptions of impairment; rather, their school participation is considered essential for two reasons. First, education itself is considered to be an ever-shifting web of relationships among all members of a community. To leave even one student out diminishes the web and reduces the learning potential and experiences of all students and teachers. Second, community is recognized as the core from which individual human possibilities and capacities are realized. One's human development does not set the conditions for community acceptance; rather, acceptance is the terrain on which development occurs. Citizenship, as I define it here, is an ongoing realization of each individual's value to the larger group.

SEEING DOWN SYNDROME: MORALITY AND
A PROFESSIONAL'S PERCEPTION

In becoming a special education instructor, I was taught to view certain human differences as abnormalities and defects that could be objectively identified, measured, and, to a degree, remediated. Initially, I did not consider it possible to question the four assumptions that form the basis of special education. As critically outlined by Bogdan and Kugelmass (1984), reiterated by Skrtic (1995a), and reflected in my own training, these underlying assumptions include: (1) Disability is a scientifically diagnosed condition that people either have or do not have; (2) objectively identifying disability and scientifically measuring its severity are possible and have educational relevance; (3) special education is a separate field from general education and involves the application of scientific principles to assist people identified as disabled; and (4) progress in special education is the result of refining assessments and interventions based on scientifically established specialized principles.

By invoking the aura of the natural sciences, a certain image of special education is created—one that suggests incremental educational advances occurring as knowledge based on experiments accumulates. *Best practices* are those teaching techniques reflective of the most current scientific understanding of disability.

The belief I held in the objectivity of disability led me, at times, to engage in questionable instructional techniques. For instance, in one early teaching experience in 1988, Melissa's mother came to school to ask that her daughter be allowed to participate in a second-grade reading group. Melissa was a 6-year-old child with Down syndrome. She attended a classroom for the *trainable mentally retarded* (referred to by teachers as the "TMR room") housed in the special education wing of a public elementary school.

I knew Melissa could read. I did not know how well because the only reading requested of children was off the calendar at circle time each morning. I assumed decoding the days of the week reflected Melissa's reading capacity. I based this belief on my general knowledge of Down syndrome and what it meant to be one of the trainable mentally retarded.

Melissa's mother, however, was persistent in her insistence that Melissa could read, and she was strong in her resistance to the special education teaching team's advice that Melissa not be set up to fail in a regular education placement. She found a second-grade teacher willing to include Melissa in a low-level reading group, and Melissa climbed the steps each morning to the second-grade classroom. Though initially shy, she was also immediately successful, and she was quickly moved to the highest-level reading group in the second grade. She was its youngest member.

The memory I have of Melissa and her reading illustrates the potentially devastating consequences of my acceptance of the objectivity of defectiveness in the education of particular children. I was unable to see past Melissa's Down syndrome to recognize her potential, her capacity, and, ultimately, her inherent right to be a part of the wider school community.

Toward a New Understanding of Disability

Following a brief teaching experience at an Illinois school segregated for children with disabilities, I had my first experience with *full inclusion* in a public elementary school in New York. Two epiphanies occurred on entering this world where children with and without disabilities attended school together. First, I quickly learned that nondisabled children did not resemble the automatrons I had imagined in my efforts to shape disabled children to look more normal. It turned out that nondisabled students had minds of their own; they were at times obnoxious, rebellious, passionate little revolutionaries. I was surrounded by miniature Che Guevaras, and I could not blame disability! No longer could revolt be labeled as a unique characteristic of disability. Certainly, my teaching instincts and solid midwestern upbringing led me to constrain the passions of childhood, but I could no longer rely on the *isolation booth* (literally solitary confinement for disruptive children) that had been a cornerstone of instructional methods at the segregated Illinois school. I had to engage these children's points of view, dialogue with them, reason, explain, and, ultimately, change myself. I came to see that teaching was as much a relationship between teacher and student as it was the dissemination of knowledge found in basal readers or the implementation of behavioral technology to punish masturbation *behaviors* during *down time* in my segregated classroom.

My second epiphany can be summarized succinctly: Students with disabilities thrived in the midst of the energy of these *regular* classrooms. Period. Certainly, their success did not come without thoughtful planning and tremendous energy on the part of teachers. But no child's success existed without these things. I was confronted by a most shocking realization: Context mattered. Physical context, intellectual context, spiritual context, instructional context, representational context—disability was shaped in the dimensions and attitudes surrounding the child's relationship to the wider world. The status of alien and squatter was not intrinsic to Down syndrome but was a consequence of the context in which the idea of Down syndrome was constructed. For instance, if I chose to use the authority of disability science to isolate children with Down syndrome into a TMR classroom that provided no meaningful literacy experiences, in essence and through the power of definition, I could create illiterate, trainable mentally retarded children. If, however, I recognized the children's right to be involved in classrooms reflective of the wider community, and if I opened up engaging literacy experiences, literate citizens would, in fact, emerge.

Together, these two epiphanies led to me to conclude that my scientific consideration of the dichotomy of normality/abnormality was not all that scientific—in fact, it seemed to have little grounding in the everyday world of children's lives. Here I taught students who could articulate Socratic questions (usually to my frustration) alongside peers whose only sounds were often difficult to interpret (yet who, I came to realize, were no less Socratic). Children with Down syndrome sat beside nondisabled children and shared in their frustration with blowing a nose or having to complete a workbook page on the days the teacher failed to prepare something more imaginative.

Certainly, these classes were not utopian. Rivalries formed, children hurt each other, some kids got left out some of the time, some days I lost my temper. But this is the experience of citizenship, and the relationships that ebbed and flowed had little to do with disability generally or with the specifics I had been trained to see as *characteristics* of defectiveness.

The Cultural Construction of Down Syndrome

The recognition that context mattered and that *defect* was not an objective aspect of a child who stood opposite normality fundamentally reoriented my interpretation of disability. This realization—that disability, Down syndrome, and the status of alien, squatter, and citizen are *cultural constructions* (S. K. Biklen, 1995)—emerged first in rudimentary form from my initial encounter with full inclusion. Based on experiences with actual children, I was forced to reject the deeply embedded functionalist assumption that social realities (such as Down syndrome) exist as objective or scientifically deduced states: The ideal student and the defective student are not fixed entities at all. Rather, they are historically situated, culturally derived perspectives in constantly shifting relationships of power and control.

Normality and impairment are not absolute categories but instead reflect cultural traditions and the current authority of certain groups, such as psychiatrists, who are charged with defining what constitutes *the differences that matter* (e.g., the APA's *Diagnostic and Statistical Manual* 1994). As discussed above, the social devaluation of people with Down syndrome to the status of alien or squatter is not inherently required; it is, rather, a choice made by people in positions of authority, and we must be held accountable.

In my segregationist teaching experiences, choices I made for my students were based on recognizing as fact their inherent defectiveness. When Melissa's mother resisted my facts through her suggestion that Melissa be allowed to read, I invoked the authority of the disability sciences in an effort to squash the small revolution: "Look, Down syndrome means mental retardation. It says so in this book, and this book, and this book. Can't you accept that?" Though Melissa's mother won the battle, the larger war raged on, and Melissa remained a member of the TMR class alienated from the wider school and from consistent reading opportunities.

Nothing inherently demanded that my own image of Melissa should carry more authority than her mother's representation. At the time, however, I firmly believed it should! The hierarchy of knowledge that emphasizes the professional's expertise in matters of disability is based on the moral sense of Down syndrome as a burden. Hence, Down syndrome becomes a social problem; as such, historically social professions have made bureaucratic and instructional efforts to scientifically contain it apart from the community.

In contrast, Melissa's mother saw her daughter as neither a social problem nor a burden. She recognized Melissa's value, worth, and humanness, and she advocated on her behalf for community access. While my form of knowledge worked to effectively separate Melissa from her general peer group, her mother's form of knowledge, which made no claim to science, sought to merge Melissa's experiences with the experiences of her non-disabled peers. In turn, this held the possibility of transforming the community in a direction that finds value in human variation.

Clearly, understanding of children, learning, and community is primarily generated in specific contexts (such as classrooms) through the relationships that we form, re-form, and refuse to form there. Though understanding emerges from these specific contexts, it is influenced by wider ongoing conversations, cultural discourses, that both constrain and potentially liberate our shared and contradictory understanding. For instance, if I had been able to shed the "disability blinders" (Goode, 1992, p. 200) imposed on my thinking by the science of disability and had been able to see Melissa through the discourse of a parent's love for her child, I too might have *discovered* her value to the community—and Melissa's school life probably would have looked quite different.

Recognizing that the multiple meanings of Down syndrome result from culturally derived, historically situated, and contextually bound definitions is antithetic to the foundational assumptions of functionalism that present Down syndrome as an objective condition with scientifically derived social consequences. Am I therefore suggesting that Down syndrome is an illusion, that its attached defects do not exist? Against the dominant traditions of disability science, that is exactly what I suggest.

Is Down Syndrome Real?

Down syndrome presents a unique opportunity for inquiry into the cultural construction of disability in schools. Its genetic etiology and recognizable phenotype are easily and often misconstrued as determinants of an objective state-of-being. Certainly, theoretical orientations that engage the cultural construction of reality do not deny human variability. We are not all the same; to suggest otherwise would be a fallacy. The genetic anomaly that expresses itself as Down syndrome creates physical and performance distinctions that begin when the father's sperm meets with the mother's oocyte (commonly called her ovum) to form a zygote—the fertilized egg that will grow into a human being (as described by Lewis, 1997).

Actually, the distinctions really begin before this in the formation of the parents' gametes, or sex cells. In order to make a gamete, a cell's usual 46 chromosomes must be split in half or else the new cell formed when parents meet would have 92 chromosomes and could not survive. Cell division requires an elegant two-step process called meiosis, which results in the formation of four sex cells, each with 23 chromosomes. However, at either one of the two meiotic points of separation, there is potential for a nondisjunction to occur. This happens when a particular chromosome, existing in combination with a twin (a homolog), fails to separate. The homolog is incorrectly maintained, meaning that one of the four gametes (sex cells) will have a double copy of a particular chromosome instead of the single copy it is now supposed to have. If this particular gamete happens to be the one that fuses with the other parent's sex cell at fertilization, the nondivided chromosome meets up with its new partner, resulting in a trisomy and a cell with 47 chromosomes.

Chromosomes form our cells' nuclei and are made up of genes strung together in intricate patterns. Genes are made up of deoxyribonucleic acids (DNA), which instruct our cells (through the mediating language of ribonucleic acid [RNA]) to manufacture particular proteins in particular ways. Proteins, in turn, are constructed from amino acids—the building blocks of life. It is within these gene structures that the particular attributes of our individuality are initially laid out, ready and willing to meet the wider world at a point of cultural dissension called the nature/nurture debate.

If nondisjunction during meiosis should occur at the gamete's 21st chromosome, the result at conception is trisomy 21 (three 21st chromosomes), commonly called Down syndrome. Mitosis (non–sex cell division) will follow the initial genetic blueprint laid out by the zygote, and every cell in the body will contain an extra 21st chromosome. This is the most common etiology of Down syndrome. However, two other chromosome 21 anomalies may occur at rare moments. At times, there may be a *translocation* of the third 21st chromosome onto another chromosome, resulting again in an extra chromosome 21 in every cell, but attached to a different chromosome pair (most commonly chromosomes 14 or 22). More rare still is nondisjunction occurring after fetal cell division has already begun. Termed mosaicism, this results in some cells with trisomy 21 and some cells without.

The DNA-based differences at the 21st chromosome result in poorly understood physical and performance differences beginning at birth and continuing throughout life. Though these genetic and physical differences are a reality outside and apart from our interpretive processes, it is the meaning we attach to the differences, the cultural constructions, that turn them into the *ones that matter* when establishing an understanding of Down syndrome.

Trisomy 21 has, ultimately, little to do with our representation of Down syndrome. Educational, social, and cultural treatments rarely make reference to a subject's karotype. For instance, not so many years ago, to have Down syndrome meant one was considered "hardly human" (Spock, 1949, p. 478) and was incarcerated in a custodial institution for life (Blatt,

1987). Nothing about anyone's genetic structure required this treatment, as is evidenced in the level of community participation enjoyed by many people with Down syndrome today (Nadel & Rosenthal, 1995). Nevertheless, warehousing human beings with the appearance of Down syndrome in decrepit environments was accepted by the majority of disability professionals through much of the twentieth century as representative of *best practices*, the pinnacle of applied achievement in the science of disability. So, to reiterate my response to the above question, yes, Down syndrome as it has generally been represented in the professional disability field is a cultural illusion.

2

Down Syndrome and the History of Community Banishment

Shelly Loveland, a 9-year-old upstate New Yorker who participated in my 2-year study on schooling and Down syndrome, had consistently experienced segregated educational options for children with disabilities throughout her school life. As a toddler, she was enrolled into a self-contained, county-sponsored early childhood program for children with multiple handicaps. She remained a part of this setting until age 5, when her largely rural, albeit wealthy, local school district directly took over the responsibility of educating Shelly. Shelly's mother, Ruth, remembered:

> We went to this meeting when Shelly was ready for kindergarten—or whatever you want to call it. The school people set it up and were very nice. It was the committee on special ed, and the people from [Shelly's early childhood program], and us, of course. Basically, we were told Shelly would transition into the class for kids with multiple disabilities, the severe program. Shelly was severely mentally retarded then. They said she had a mental age of like a year, which seemed totally ridiculous, but what did we know? Kids like Shelly went to the severe room. That was it. That's where they told us she'd receive the individual attention she needed.

The presumption that Shelly and other children considered to be like her require segregation from the wider school community is currently justified in the disability literature on scientific, psychological, and benevolent grounds as an advance in the treatment of human variation (Lieberman, 1996). In tracing the history of segregation, however, it becomes clear that current practices of school exclusion are rooted in distinctly nonscientific cultural traditions of banishing those who do not conform to socially prescribed, functional standards of the ideal citizen. Whether they have

19

been labeled "mad," "idiotic," "evil," "moronic," or "mentally retarded," people who appear to deviate from the norm have been caught in a history of community exclusion.

THE ORIGINS OF BANISHMENT

Western school practices that confine students with Down syndrome and other disabilities to the status of alien and squatter can be traced back several centuries to a transformation of the social meaning of human variation in both Christian and scientific sensibilities. The change in cultural imagery was brought about by the Reformation and Scientific Revolution. Foucault (1965) described the consequences of this transition in understanding as a shift from *embarkation* to *confinement*.

Medieval Embarkation

Through the first quarter of the sixteenth century, banishment for people perceived as mentally deviant did at times take the form of custodial imprisonment, resulting in the status of the alien confined from the community. (Note, for instance, the construction in Hamburg in 1376 of the "Idiot's Cage," a prison tower for social outcasts described by Scheerenberger [1983].) However, the prevailing discourse of the age positioned *madness*, a term capturing multiple constituents of the *unreasonable mind*, in an existential location of unworldliness (Foucault, 1965). Unreason existed on the murky geographic horizon that served as a border to civilized lands inhabited by the Reasonable.

In this medieval interpretation of difference, banishment took the form of embarkation (Foucault, 1965). Unreason was separated from Reason through the act of driving away those who did not conform to community citizenship standards. The ultimate manifestation of this alienation was the Ship of Fools—literally vessels filled with the Unreasonable set adrift on the sea. Certainly, the practice of driving madness into the oceans served a utilitarian function in that communities would not have to divert social and material resources to the care of burdensome individuals; yet this functional dimension appeared secondary to the rite of passage reserved for those whose true homeland it was believed existed "only in that fruitless expanse between two countries" (Foucault, 1965, p. 11).

From Embarkation to Confinement: The Emergence of the Animal

The Reformation and Scientific Revolution altered cultural attitudes toward Unreason. Increasingly, the image of *economic* burden and its association with evil became attached to deviance. Martin Luther himself has been quoted on the need to remove deviants from the community in the harshest of manners. In 1644, he encountered a 12-year-old boy who, according to Luther, only "ate, defecated, and drooled and, if anyone tackled him, screamed. If things didn't go well, he wept. . . . [He was] merely a mass of flesh, a massa carnis, with no soul" (Luther, 1652/1959, quoted in Kanner, 1964, p. 7). Luther's diagnosis: The child and those like him were possessed by the devil. His recommendation: immediate drowning.

Though Luther may have been misquoted (Blatt, 1987), there can be no doubt that a shift in the discourse on deviancy occurred with the cultural and economic changes brought on by the Reformation. Folly—human foolishness, unreasonableness, and mental and spiritual vacuity—rose through the hierarchy of human vices to a position of prominence. Folly lost its link to the geographic horizons and was firmly established as an inhabitant of the mind and soul: "Madness no longer lies in wait at the four corners of the Earth; it insinuates itself within Man" (Foucault, 1965, p. 26). Folly came to be closely associated with the social problems of poverty, crime, prostitution, and disease that appeared alongside industrialization and the expansion of European cities. It was assigned oppositional status to the moral obligation of work and to the ethical value of labor.

In the seventeenth century, the discourse on banishment firmly shifted from embarkation to community burden and confinement. Across Europe, people whose utilitarian value was in question were quarantined in newly formed institutions in per capita numbers not seen since leprosy had been conquered 200 years earlier. In 1656, the Hôpital Général opened in Paris as a series of institutions to confine those who failed to integrate themselves into the community (Scheerenberger, 1983). Though referred to as a *hospital*, the Hôpital Général was, in effect, a prison: "One thing is clear: the Hôpital Général is not a medical establishment. It is rather a sort of semijudicial structure, an administrative entity which, along with the already constituted powers [of confinement], and outside the courts, decides, judges, and executes" (Foucault, 1965, p. 40).

Those charged as economic burdens existed in the most decrepit of conditions: chained at the neck, behind bars, strewn on feces-soaked hay, stacked together by the dozen in tiny cells, and at times placed on display for the community's entertainment (Scheerenberger, 1983). In the theological notions of the day, such treatment was not considered harsh. The inmates were, after all, a species separate from humanity—a form of animal, not human at all. This discourse of animality (Foucault, 1965), originally existing apart from science, would take a prominent position in the scientific interpretation of disability that emerged in the nineteenth century (see below).

Down Syndrome Through the Discourse of Animality

The existence of people with trisomy 21 prior to the nineteenth century
is uncertain. The medical dilemmas associated with Down syndrome, including circulatory and respiratory distress, clearly hindered survival.
However, evidence points to the appearance of chromosomal anomalies
early on in the evolution of the human species. In the 1970s, gorillas and
chimpanzees were reported with nondisjunctions resulting in trisomony
21, suggesting that its occurrence in human beings originated prior to the
moment our evolutionary path split from that of the apes (Bérubé, 1996).
    Actual evidence of people with trisomy 21 prior to the nineteenth
century is elusive. No *clear* written accounts of what would later be termed
Down syndrome exist prior to Robert Chambers's (1844/1890, p. 309) reference to a "Mongolian type—that is, persons who in maturity still are a
kind of children" and Edouard Seguin's 1846 notation of a subclass of cretinism he termed "furfuraceous idiocy," referring to the subjects' dry and
peeling skin (see Seguin, 1866/1907, p. 32).
    In paintings, depictions of people with features associated with Down
syndrome have appeared sporadically throughout history. In the fifteenth
century Andrea Mantegna created a series of paintings of the Madonna
with Child in which the infant's face and body have particular characteristics common to Down syndrome (Ruhräh, 1935). In 1618, Christ may again
have been depicted as having trisomy 21 in the *Adoration of the Shepherds*,
a painting by the Flemish artist Jacob Jordeans (Volpe, 1986). The significance of Christ as a child with disabilities is unknown. Perhaps the depic-
tions represent a Renaissance interpretation of Unreason as the ultimate
source of truth—only those who existed as its opposite could ever honestly
know Reason (Foucault, 1965). Perhaps they represent an aesthetic effort
to capture innocence, though innocence was not firmly associated with
disability until the mid-twentieth century.
    In 1773, Sir Joshua Reynolds painted *Lady Cockburn and Her Children*,
in which one child appears to display characteristics of Down syndrome
(Volpe, 1986). This claim, however, has been summarily dismissed: "Such
a diagnosis would be grossly inaccurate, as it is known that the child later
grew up to be an admiral of the British fleet" (Volpe, 1986, p. 427). Volpe's
twentieth-century sensibilities of the limitations of Down syndrome are
broadly projected onto the occupational potentials of particular people who
may have had trisomy 21 in the eigtheenth and nineteenth centuries.
    The lack of a disability category specific to trisomy 21 throughout
much of history probably stems from two sources. First, we know today
that the performance capabilities of people with Down syndrome vary
considerably. Certain people with Down syndrome appear quite able to

conform to school and community standards of behavior and intellect, while others demonstrate a range of dilemmas in conforming to the norms of the group. Those who do conform, though, remain stigmatized in modern times by their appearance and its symbolic value as a banner for incompetence (see Chapter 3). In the past, appearance had less impact on spoiling one's everyday identity than it does today (Taylor & Searl, 1987). If one could perform the labor of the day, there was no need for separation from the community into a category of defect. Such separation into *mild*, or *high-incidence*, classifications is a twentieth-century phenomenon (Sarason & Doris, 1979). Perhaps Lady Cockburn's child did have trisonomy 21, but in such a manner that his military competence was unaffected, or even affected in a positive (militaristic) direction. Why, then, should the British Navy not seek his services?

The second reason for the historical lack of a distinct Down syndrome category is commonly cited: People with Down syndrome were probably considered cretins (Benda, 1960; Down, 1887/1990; Volpe, 1986). Cretinism was a congenital form of the broader classification of idiocy initially recognized in the seventeenth century (Scheerenberger, 1983). The physical appearances of people considered to be cretins and those with what would later be termed Down syndrome were similar. Thus the two were fused as a single condition (Benda, 1960).

THE DELINEATION OF DOWN SYNDROME
IN THE GENESIS OF POSITIVISM

Improved nutrition and a developing understanding of the effects of iodine on the thyroid gland diminished the incidence of endemic cretinism in Europe throughout the eighteenth and nineteenth centuries (Volpe, 1986). However, the trisonomy at the 21st chromosome did not respond to these nutritional or medical advances. This resulted in a higher percentage of people with trisonomy 21 forming the category of cretinism and probably led, in conjunction with the rise of positivist human sciences (see below), to Chambers's and Seguin's initial distinction of the "Mongolian type" and "furfuraceous idiocy."

Though both Chambers and Seguin exerted considerable influence on the interpretation of deviance in the nineteenth century, their references to what would come to be termed Down syndrome are a mere footnote in the history of the chromosomal anomaly. Most sources point to 1866 as the pivotal year for distinguishing Down syndrome as a *discovered* category of disability. It was in this year that the English physician John Langdon Hayes Down published a paper in the *London Hospital Reports and Observations* that arranged people considered idiots into a racial hierarchy of competence. Down based his analysis on physical characteristics that he felt resembled the features of ethnic and racial groups considered to be evolutionarily beneath the presumed Caucasian pinnacle of development. In an 1887 extension of his earlier essay, Dr. Down wrote:

> I have for some time had my attention directed to the possibility of making a classification of the feeble-minded, by arranging them around various ethnic standards—in other words, framing a natural system to supplement the information to be derived by an inquiry into the history of the case.
>   I have been able to find among the large number of idiots and imbeciles . . . that a considerable portion can be fairly referred to one of the great divisions of the human family other than the class from which they have sprung. (1887/1990, p. 128)

Among the ethnic varieties of feeble-mindedness identified, including Ethiopian and Malaysian constituents, Down described representatives from "the great Mongolian family," who, a century later, would come to be labeled as having Down syndrome. He noted:

> A very large number of congenital idiots are typical Mongols. So marked in this, that when placed side by side, it is difficult to believe that the specimens compared are not children of the same parents. (1887/1990, p. 129)

In describing one "idiot member of this [Mongolian] racial division," Down (1887/1990) wrote:

> The boy's aspect is such, that it is difficult to realize that he is the child of Europeans; but so frequently are these characters presented, that there can be no doubt that these ethnic features are the result of degeneration. (p. 129)

Down's medical contention of evolutionary degeneration occurring in the offspring of European parents merged the discourse of animality with the doctrines of scientific positivism on which psychology would form its mechanistic base.

The Rise of Positivism and Its Influences on Human Understanding

The effects of the Scientific Revolution, beginning, arguably, in the sixteenth century, influenced all of Western culture, in part through the influential writings of intellectuals such as Francis Bacon (1561–1626) and René Descartes (1596–1650). In 1637 Descartes published his *Discourse on Method*, in which he philosophically split the spiritual world (the mind) from the physical world (the body) and argued that all aspects of the latter could only be interpreted and understood through mathematical deduction (see Descartes, 1637/1951). Francis Bacon urged intellectuals to pursue new knowledge through methodological observation and experimental research, thus formalizing an empiricist, seemingly atheoretical, approach to discovering truth (see Bacon, 1605–1627/1952).

The ideas of Descartes and Bacon merged to create (1637/1952) the standard for the scientific method and influenced the Enlightenment writings of social thinkers who sought to apply the natural truths emerging from science to procure technologies for the advancement of civilized society. In the first half of the nineteenth century, Auguste Comte adapted the reasoning of science specifically to the understanding of social interaction and human society.

Comte believed that all knowledge passed through an evolutionary hierarchy beginning with theological (or fictitious) understanding, followed by metaphysical (or abstract) understanding, and finally reaching its pinnacle with scientific (or positive) understanding (see Schön, 1983). He traced this intellectual evolution in the histories of astronomy, physics, and chemistry, and concluded that positivist methods would eventually lead to the discovery of eternal laws of human relations. This would, in turn, allow scientists to impose the laws of human harmony onto less enlightened individuals and groups.

The Impact of Evolution on Interpreting Human Beings

Comte's evolutionary metaphor of sociointellectual development was no accident, nor were its connotations neutral. It reflected a growing social fascination in the 1800s with emerging theories of natural selection and insight into the origins of humankind. Darwin's 1859 treatise *On the Origin of Species by the Means of Natural Selection* described for the first time the principle of "the survival of the fittest" (see Darwin, 1859/1963). Of course, Darwin's work profoundly influenced the biological sciences, but it also influenced the cultural and anthropological understanding of human behavior.

Prior to the application of Darwinian evolution to the understanding of particular people and groups of people (Social Darwinism), degeneration, or the reversion of individuals to lower forms of life, had been advanced as a cause of human abnormality. In 1857, the French physician Benedict Augustin Morel published a treatise on the "stigmata of degeneration" in which he argued that cretinism was the final manifestation of several generations of perverse living (see Gelb, 1995). Each subsequent generation up to the cretin was more feeble than the preceding one, demonstrating in observable, empirical form the wrath of God.

Degeneracy was presumed to scientifically confirm Original Sin (Gelb, 1995; Pick, 1989).

Following Darwin's insight into the processes of natural selection, theories of degeneration were cloaked in the language of the emergent evolutionary sciences. Those who supported evolutionary degeneracy, including J. Langdon Down, hypothesized that "degenerates were atavistic reversions to earlier [evolutionary] stages, living fossils who provided a window into the past" (Gelb, 1995, p. 3). The belief was based, in part, on the assumption that individual development, a child's growth into adulthood, actually proceeded through the various stages of evolutionary development. Chambers (1844/1890) explained:

> Our brain goes through the various stages of a fish's, a reptile's and a mammifier's brain, and finally becomes human. There is more than this, for, after completing the animal transformation, it passes through the characters in which it appears, in the Negro, Malay, American, and Mongolian nations and finally is Caucasian. (p. 306)

Each person was seen as representing a miniature version of the entire biological progression of the species. For some, including people with Down syndrome, development was thought to have been arrested at a particular stage beneath what was seen as the Caucasian pinnacle.

In the nineteenth century, then, several discourses merged to produce a basis for interpreting disability, including Down syndrome, and for its consequential treatment. The Reformation took a dim view of those who did not clearly partake in the labor of the community. Banishment for those deemed to be community burdens took the form of confinement. Confinement occurred in decrepit institutions based on the abstract justification that those so banished were animals, a lower species in relation to humanity. Ideas of evolution, born out of the Scientific Revolution and applied in a positivistic effort to understand human beings, reconfigured the discourse of animality to one of scientific degeneracy while retaining banishment as a central consequence.

A MOMENT OF HOPE: THE IDEA OF EDUCABILITY

In the nineteenth century, as the category of Down syndrome emerged, confinement retained its prominent position as the treatment for representatives of evolutionary degeneracy. However, certain educators and social thinkers, also inspired by Enlightenment philosophies, resisted banishment as the natural consequence of difference. Jean-Marc-Gaspard Itard, a French

physician, believed strongly in Jean-Jacques Rousseau's enlightened philosophy that human beings unfold, or develop, according to natural laws.
The concept of degeneration, of course, sprang from a similar belief but
was tinged with hopelessness. Itard, however, found hope in the idea that
by using the laws of human development, those who strayed from nature's
path could be educated in a more appropriate direction.

Viewed through a twentieth-century lens, Itard's pedagogical methods are commonly mistaken by current special education professionals as
the precursor to behavior modification. Itard's educational efforts, however, were very much rooted in a firm belief that learning resulted from a
student's active agency under the guidance of a thoughtful instructor, an
idea antithetical to behaviorism's perception of the passive student react-
ing to schedules of reinforcement and punishment controlled by the teacher.
While Itard's ideas can be traced back to Rousseau, behaviorism finds its
roots in Locke's view of the newborn as a *tabula rasa*.

Itard's methodology directly reflected the writings of the Abbé de
Condillac, a French intellectual who believed that the senses were the
agents of the mind's ideas (H. Lane, 1979). Itard applied Condillac's *sensu-
alist* ideas in his efforts to educate Victor, the famed Wild Boy of Aveyron
who was found wandering the French woods. Victor, named by Itard, was
considered by most educational authorities of the time to be uneducable.
However, Itard felt that by engaging Victor in planful experiences, the
child's senses would develop into a civilized form leading to normal
thought processes. Over the course of 5 years, Itard became increasingly
frustrated with Victor's lack of progress despite the child's development
of writing skills and other educational triumphs. Though Itard expressed
distress, other French educators were both awed and humbled by Victor's
successes. The discourse of educability of the *uneducable* emerged.

Itard's pedagogical methods were brought to the United States in the
mid-nineteenth century by his most famous disciple, Edouard (changed
to Edward) Seguin. Seguin reinterpreted Itard's work, as well as the writings of other intellectuals, into a *physiological education*. In this form, Seguin
claimed, idiots could be taught through three instructional emphases:
muscular education, sensory education, and moral education (Seguin,
1866/1907).

Seguin believed that strict banishment and separation of individuals
with disabilities into locations apart from the wider community exacerbated
their differences. Instead, education should occur in association with nondisabled people in churches, museums, parks, and theaters; it should focus
on the development of useful skills needed to perform necessary community tasks (Seguin, 1866/1907, p. 169). At the same time, and somewhat in
contradiction, Seguin relied on central locations as instructional sites at

which his physiological education could be efficiently undertaken. This resulted in the emergence and eventual proliferation of institutions.

THE REEMERGENCE OF HOPELESSNESS: EUGENICS AND THE PROFESSION OF DISABILITY

The Civil War and a severe economic depression beginning in 1873 led to a transition in the purpose of the institution: from a Seguinian site for educating people with disabilities to a custodial warehouse. Families, charities, and the state suffered a crisis in their ability to care for and educate the increasing numbers of individuals considered to be economic liabilities. The shift back to banishment through absolute confinement eliminated Seguin's pedagogy, on which the proliferation of institutions had been based. Ironically, this late-nineteenth-century reversion occurred at the very moment when the occupations concerned with what were deemed *social problems* sought legitimacy as professions.

Professional credibility rested on Comte's positivist assumption that scientific laws could be deduced that would lead to occupational techniques that bettered humanity. The three tenets of professionalism included (1) an underlying basic science on which was built and (2) an applied science that resulted in (3) a practical set of clinical and occupational skills (Schein, 1972, cited in Schön, 1983). The elimination of the educational purpose of institutions resulted in a foundational vacuum. Confinement became a *moral* response to the social problem of those construed to be burdens, not a scientific endeavor—thus, not a professional one either. If those charged with the care and control of community burdens were to gain the status of professionals, some form of objective knowledge tradition had to be slipped beneath the structure of the institution.

Eugenics and Professional Credibility

Eugenics emerged at the end of the nineteenth century as the positivistic foundation for professionalizing banishment through confinement. Changes in American society brought on by new immigration patterns that resulted in an influx of Eastern Europeans merged with industrialization, the rise of cities, and the consequences of capitalism, leading to cultural instability similar to that experienced in Europe following the Reformation and Scientific Revolution. Social philosophers and intellectuals responded to societal concerns with crime, vice, immorality, and pauperism much as the Europeans had done: by linking these social problems to human variation. Specifically, the construct of mental deficiency, or feeble-mindedness, was blamed for America's cultural ills (Winship, 1900).

The "science of eugenics" proposed that the solution to cultural problems would come with better human breeding. This meant the control and
ultimate elimination of what was considered poor human stock. Henry
Goddard (1914), director of the research laboratory of the Training School
for Feeble-Minded Girls and Boys at Vineland, New Jersey, explained:

> The large share of attention which has been given to the new science of eu-
> genics, or race betterment, shows conclusively that society is intensely inter-
> ested in this problem of the improvement of the race. . . . The feeble-minded
> person is not desirable, he is a social encumbrance, often a burden to him-
> self. In short it were better both for him and for society had he never been
> born. Should we not then, in our attempt to improve the race, begin by pre-
> venting the birth of more feeble-minded? (p. 558)

Eugenics represented a discourse of disability merging a triad of what
were then considered *scientific advances*: Social Darwinism, hereditary sta-
tistics, and psychometrics (Kliewer & Drake, 1998). According to the nineteenth-century Social Darwinists, who drew from ideas of evolutionary
degeneracy, a human social order arranged hierarchically existed not just
across cultures but within a single society. Stratification was governed by
the same natural principles that bounded the biological order. Herbert Spencer, a nineteenth-century social philosopher, referred to the natural law of
"the survival of the fittest" as the basis for a society's stratified social order:
"The poor," according to Spencer, "were the ill-fated weak, the prosperous
the chosen strong" (quoted in McKay, Hill, & Buckler, 1983, p. 868).

Along with Social Darwinism, the creation of numerical models thought
to scientifically demonstrate the wide variation of human characteristics
across groups, but stability over generations, combined with Mendelian
genetics to focus attention on what was believed to be the inheritance of
feeble-mindedness in the poor classes. Goddard (1914) noted that "since
feeble-mindedness is in all probability transmitted in accordance with the
Mendelian Law of heredity, the way is open for eugenic procedure which
shall mean much for the future welfare of the race" (p. 509). Goddard and
other eugenicists published *pedigree studies*, presented as science, purport-
edly tracing generations of particular impoverished families in order to demonstrate the societal menace of *familial* feeble-mindedness (J. D. Smith, 1985).

Social Darwinism and statistical models of familial idiocy merged with
the third prong of eugenics, psychometrics, during a trip Goddard made
to Europe in 1908. While visiting France, Goddard encountered a test created by Alfred Binet and Théodore Simon that appeared to measure what
was described as students' *mental ages*.

Though Binet and Simon did not suggest that their test measured
some stable level of general intelligence (Blatt, 1987), Goddard returned

to the United States claiming just that (Goddard, 1914). He, along with Lewis Terman and other test devisers, developed measurements of intellect, the *science* of psychometrics, that were used to separate out for control purposes people thought to be a menace to society. Using circular logic that would remain an entrenched aspect of IQ testing throughout the twentieth century (Singham, 1995), the eugenicists pointed to their own assessments, normed on culturally and economically established groups of Americans, as objective evidence that particular categories of people just arriving in America were cognitively deficient and required segregation from a community at risk of cultural upheaval (Kliewer & Drake, 1998). In doing so, Goddard (1914) literally generated an entirely new category of *high-functioning* feeble-mindedness, which he called the "moron" (p. 4).

While the categories of the idiot and the imbecile, which encompassed mongoloids and others considered to have severe disabilities, were distinguishable prior to the new psychometric testing, morons, Goddard claimed, were dangerous precisely because they looked so normal. Yet they were morally corrupt and would ultimately bring about the downfall of American society unless identified through psychometrics in order that they could be weeded out and controlled by the professions so charged.

Eugenics and the Proliferation of Confinement

The professions associated with the control of people with disabilities profited tremendously from the idea of better breeding. Eugenics lent scientific credibility to the proliferation and expansion of systems of confinement resulting in a greatly expanded base of power, privilege, and authority from which to further promote segregationist advances. The methodology of control primarily took form in the expansion of the institution, the use of forced sterilization, and the emergence of special education (Sarason & Doris, 1969).

Goddard was awed by the immensity of the task of institutionalizing the growing numbers of people psychometrics identified as societal menaces. He noted that "that would mean 1000 colonies of 300 each. . . . From 2 to 30 institutions in each state according to population" (1914, p. 582). The number of institutions as well as the size of the existing institutions were increasing dramatically, but these institutions could not contain the vast throngs of people eugenically identified as requiring banishment.

In 1917, Goddard claimed that up to 50% of all new immigrants coming through Ellis Island were feeble-minded (Trent, 1994). The eugenicists and institution superintendents looked to forced sterilization of people identified through psychometrics as an alternative form of control (Sarason

& Doris, 1969). They also looked to the public school system as an ally in confining the feeble-minded (Sarason & Doris, 1969, 1979).

The Eugenic Impact on Schooling: The Emergence of Special Education

The first segregated classrooms for children defined as disabled appeared at the end of the nineteenth century in conjunction with the developing eugenics movement and compulsory school attendance laws. While children with Down syndrome were automatically excluded from educational options based on their presumed inability to learn, the earliest segregated classrooms concerned themselves with *slow and backward* students, the morons, who were, by law, entering the public school system.

The moronic students were the offspring of the new immigrants from southern and Eastern Europe. They demonstrated difficulty with the English language and American cultural customs: "From the time that special classes began, they were largely populated by 'subculture' children from minority groups" (Sarason & Doris, 1979, p. 6). Trent (1994) pointed out that one of the earliest segregated classrooms, created in Chicago in 1895, was populated by "backward" children, "most of whom were immigrants having difficulties in the public schools" (p. 146). In 1921, 75% of the children in New York City's special education system were of foreign-born parentage and were preponderantly children of the poor (Sarason & Doris, 1979).

Down Syndrome and the Science of Eugenics

Down's 1866 delineation of a mongol category of idiocy was basically ignored for a decade. In 1876, however, Fraser and Mitchell published a paper in the *Journal of Mental Science* that described 62 cases of "Kalmuc idiocy." The term *Kalmuc* came from the Kalmuck people, a group of Mongolians who had migrated to Russia. Though Fraser and Mitchell did not cite Down's work, they reiterated his belief that the syndrome described was a manifestation of evolutionary degeneracy. In 1877, Ireland published his influential text *On Idiocy and Imbecility*, in which he created 12 categories of disability. Included among these was the mongolian idiot, a classification Ireland positioned as distinct from the cretinoid. At the birth of eugenics, Down syndrome was firmly established as a unique disability type.

The eugenic creation of segregated special education was most concerned with identifying and controlling the moron. At the turn of the century, educators and medical personnel agreed with Dr. Down that his syndrome represented a single point of severe retardation afflicting all who were so classified. Goddard (1914) noted, "It is a remarkable fact that the mentality of mongolian imbeciles is almost always that of a four-year-old child" (p. 453).

This image of severe impairment precluded the need for public school special educators to concern themselves with the mongol child. Family care and confinement in an institution were seen as natural consequences of the disability. Kerr (1926), in describing people with Down syndrome, noted, "The mental type is low. . . . They are often echolalic, and have defective speech, forming consonants badly; reading and writing are beyond their powers. . . . The diagnosis of typical mongolism ought to be clear, and when made is hopeless for educational improvement . . . they never cease to be imbeciles" (p. 396).

Despite this image of hopelessness, Down (1887/1990) himself had acknowledged Seguin's pedagogical success with educating the *uneducable*, and he noted that people described as mongoloid

> very much repay judicious treatment. . . . They have considerable power of imitation, even bordering on being mimics. They are humorous, and a lively sense of the ridiculous often colours their mimicry. This faculty of imitation may be cultivated to a very great extent, and a practical direction given to the results obtained. They are usually able to speak; the speech is thick and indistinct, but may be improved very greatly by a well-directed scheme of tongue gymnastics. The coordination faculty is abnormal, but not so defective that it cannot be greatly strengthened. By systematic training, considerable manipulative power may be obtained. (p. 130)

However optimistic Down's perceptions may appear in light of the eugenic claim to hopelessness, he maintained a belief that institutions were the only proper location for people with disabilities: "Association with their superiors condemns them to a life of isolation which renders nugatory all efforts for their improvement" (Down, 1887/1990, p. 132).

The Discourse of Variability. Though the eugenic perception of a monolithic intellectual type perpetuated the need for institutionalizing individuals with Down syndrome, a competing discourse of variability within the classification, based in part on Down's argument for "judicious treatment," was emerging (see Booth, 1985). Still (1909, p. 538, as cited in Booth, 1985) noted: "Some of the highest grade mongols can be taught to read simple words and even write after a fashion." Tredgold (1929, p. 223, as cited in Booth, 1985) explained that "the milder grades . . . learn to read, write and perform simple duties with a considerable amount of intelligence." Crookshank (1931) made the dramatic claim that "we should not suppose idiocy or imbecility to be a necessary concomitant or ingredient of 'mongolism'" (p. 13).

Although Crookshank's statement appears to shatter all previous understanding of Down syndrome, it was made within his eugenic text *The Mongol in Our Midst*. He wrote this book to warn of the impending cultural cataclysm that would result if white society did not purify its blood of the contaminants of degeneration. In essence, he positioned the mongol alongside the moron as an equal societal menace.

The Demise of Overt Eugenics

Of interest to the understanding of Down syndrome, Crookshank's treatise was published at a point in the twentieth century when overt American eugenics was generally in demise. The effects of eugenics, however, would have consequences for students with Down syndrome and other disabilities extending to the end of the millennium.

Beginning in the 1920s, confidence in eugenics fell victim to a number of factors. Medical personnel, who had been supportive of the nonmedical, psychometrically oriented eugenicists, feared their own authority was dissipating while that of the psychologist was on the rise (Trent, 1994). Psychiatry as a profession began to withdraw its support in favor of a new model of mental deviance referred to as the "mental hygiene movement." This movement rejected the large custodial institutions in favor of a more community-based set of services, such as psychodynamic, Freudian therapies through which individuals could resolve their psychic conflicts. This new focus resulted in a waning psychiatric interest in developmental disabilities.

Sarason and Doris (1969) suggest that eugenics was dealt a serious blow by the Great Depression and the resulting New Deal. The disrupted lives of millions of Americans suggested that individuals might, at times, be victims of forces beyond their control; rather than deserving community scorn, Americans needed systems of support. This shift in attitude affected the perception of people with disabilities, who also might be thought of as victims rather than menaces.

Also, World War II resulted in conscientious objectors performing community service at state institutions. They were shocked at the horrific conditions in these institutions and, in turn, joined the growing movement of reformers who saw people with disabilities as victims requiring protection from a harsh society (Trent, 1994).

Added to these elements was an emerging *parents' movement* (Shapiro, 1994) around issues of disability following World War II. During the eugenics movement, feeble-mindedness had been tied directly to poverty and pauperism. Following World War II, middle-class and upper-class families admitted that disability was a part of their lives as well. Trent (1994) described the emergence in American literature of a "parent-confessional genre" in which well-to-do families published autobiographical accounts of raising children with disabilities (e.g., P. S. Buck, 1950).

With the demise of eugenics, institutions and, to a lesser extent, special education faced a foundational crisis of professionalism. The practice of confinement no longer had a legitimizing scientific claim. With tragic irony, the positivistic vacuum would be filled with a new form of confinement as a result of the moral efforts of the parents' movement.

THE PARENTS' MOVEMENT AND BEHAVIORISM

Following World War II, parents came together to organize for educational opportunities for their children with significant disabilities. These children, including children with Down syndrome, had been excluded from the earlier version of segregated special education, with its emphasis on containing morons—children from minority cultures.

The parents' movement of the 1940s and 1950s was the first organized and sustained demand outside of the professional disability fields to expand services. That parents found their voice in the midst of a foundational vacuum in the profession of confinement (brought about with the demise of eugenics) is probably no accident. Though the entrenched segregated system of control could be justified as a protective arrangement for people now viewed as victims, this was hardly a scientific foundation on which to legitimate and perpetuate the professions that had gained prominence through identifying and controlling individuals considered to be societal menaces. Confinement had become, in effect, the trunk and branches of a tree with no roots (Kliewer & Drake, 1998).

The parental demand that educational options be developed for children previously left out of schools resulted in a new science of disability that replaced eugenics as the foundation of segregated practices. The children around whom the parents' movement rallied had consistently been excluded from educational opportunities because of the presumed degree of their inherent lack of utility. Within the professions, there was a logic to this exclusion. It was assumed that these people could not benefit from schooling and, based on intellectual vacuity, did not belong in the community. However, parental demand challenged the field's logic, resulting in an emergent interest in operant psychology.

The Emergence of Operant Psychology as Confinement

Though related to earlier behavioral learning theories (e.g., Thorndike's psychology), Skinnerian conditioning focused attention on the probability of operants (behaviors) occurring through selective reinforcement

(Dembo, 1988). If, through laboratory conditioning, rats could be made to perform in particular ways, then, according to conventions of the time, surely people with disabilities could also have their performance shaped in a utilitarian direction. For parents demanding educational options for their children who, the disability fields presumed, could not think, B. F. Skinner and his collaborators presented an ideal response.

Sobsey and Dreimanis (1993) point to an experiment conducted in 1949 as the first use of operant conditioning on an individual with a disability. In this test, Fuller sought to have an 18-year-old "vegetative human organism" raise his right hand. The young man was denied food for 15 hours. Then, when he raised his hand, sweetened milk was injected into his mouth. This selective reinforcement resulted, over time, in an increased number of right-hand movements. Fuller (1949) concluded:

> While of normal human parentage, this organism was, behaviorally speaking, considerably lower in the scale than the majority of infra-human organisms used in conditioning experiments—dogs, rats, cats. . . . Perhaps by beginning at the bottom of the human scale the transfer from rat to man can be effected. (p. 590)

Fuller's experiment led in the 1950s to an invigorated research effort to condition the behaviors of people considered disabled (Berkson & Landesman-Dwyer, 1977). Initially termed "the experimental analysis of behavior," this effort quickly turned specifically toward what its proponents considered socially important behaviors and was renamed "applied behavior analysis" (Baer, Wolf, & Risley, 1968, 1987).

Operant psychology under any name served important functions for the disability fields. It combined with psychometrics to reestablish an empiricist knowledge foundation in the tradition of Comte, which had been lacking after the demise of eugenics. While psychometric measures had continued to separate students into already existing segregated environments, behavior modification now served the segregated classrooms as an actual justification for their existence.

In the form of a human science, operant psychology maintained the status of technically trained professionals as the ultimate experts on disability. Since its purposes were the prediction and control of behavior, the power differential was reinforced between instructors and students: The teacher was charged with deciding which behavior would be conditioned to what end, and students were identified as passive respondents to the influence exerted by a controlled environment.

Operant conditioning supported the continuation and expansion of the segregated systems of control by equating human beings with the laboratory animals on whom this brand of learning theory was developed. Such an equation justified the removal of students with disabilities from the unpredictability of regular lives:

> In order to apply the laboratory science of behaviorism to special education, it was necessary to model the special education classroom after the laboratory rather than the regular classroom. The highly controlled conditions that were considered to be necessary for teaching students with special needs were alien to and incompatible with regular classrooms. The results have been catastrophic for students of special education. (Sobsey & Dreimanis, 1993, p. 5)

Scant evidence existed then or now that skills taught in segregated classrooms based on behavior modification principles generalized to the wider community. This lack of generalizability required that a further set of rigid environments be maintained into which students schooled in segregated classrooms could transition. Similar to the eugenic logic of the institution as the natural outcome of special education, laboratory-like classrooms utilizing extrinsic foci of control perpetuated the need for institutions. Hence institutions retained their rigid, controlling identity, justified now by the pedagogical claims of operant psychology.

With no model for schooling children with severe disabilities in existence apart from the institution and early forms of ungraded classrooms, the parents' movement viewed the rise in self-contained schools and classrooms as progress. In fact, the majority of schools for students with disabilities were begun through the efforts of parents (Shapiro, 1994). Here, finally, was a location cloaked in an educational aura that welcomed their children in the midst of wider community revulsion.

Contesting Representations of Down Syndrome Within the Parents' Movement

The parents' movement resulted in a new form of educational confinement viewed then as progressive for students with disabilities. However, children with Down syndrome, still trapped in increasingly shaky assumptions of degeneration, initially struggled to gain admittance. Spock, in an early edition of his influential and generally insightful text on baby and child care, voiced support for raising children with disabilities at home and schooling them in appropriate programs. However, he had a different prescription for children with Down syndrome. Spock (1949) advised parents of newborn *mongoloid* infants to immediately institutionalize them, explaining that the child would "exist at a level that is hardly human," thereby wrenching apart the social fabric of the family (p. 478).

Weingold (1953), an early leader in the parents' movement and founder of the New York Association for the Help of Retarded Children (which separated from the National Association for Retarded Children, a parent-led organization that would later become the ARC), struggled to find a school that would educate his son, Johnny, with Down syndrome.

Despite Weingold's prominent status in the community and Johnny's early development of literacy skills, several special schools rejected the child on sight. Personnel presumed that a person with Down syndrome was inherently educationally hopeless. Eventually, one school acquiesced to Weingold's wishes and admitted Johnny. But the school refused to place him in the *regular special* section, instead relegating him to the *low-grade option*. Weingold fought this presumption to no avail until he finally secured a letter to the school from the well-known Down syndrome researcher Clemens E. Benda: "It was only after a classic letter by Dr. Benda on the equal rights of all races, Asiatic as well as Caucasian, to public education that Johnny was admitted to the regular special class" (Weingold, 1953, p. 254).

The continuing strong connection of Down syndrome to degeneration, hopelessness, and social scorn stood in opposition to the intense desire on the part of the parents' movement to gain respectability and community space for children with severe disabilities. This dichotomy resulted in the separation of people with Down syndrome from other groups of excluded people around whom the parents' movement rallied.

Resistance to the Discourse of the Ultimate Alien

The parents' movement representation of people with Down syndrome as the ultimate alien was not without its detractors. In 1953, the popular TV and movie star Dale Evans Rogers, married to Roy Rogers, published *Angel Unaware*, an account of the brief life of their daughter Robin, born with Down syndrome. Though Rogers (1953) portrayed Down syndrome as an "appalling handicap" and sympathized with parents who institutionalized their babies, she nonetheless counseled raising all children in the home (p. 7).

That same year Rosenzweig (1953), drawing on the discourse of variability, systematized a three-tiered hierarchy of Down syndrome that ran from hopelessness to limited utilitarian value. The lowest category, termed "the dependents," was made up of "those children who, because of a combination and a degree of mental defect, emotional instability, social immaturity, physical defect, academic disability, and a poor or inadequate 'drive,' present a continuing and lasting failure to compete successfully in social or vocational pursuits" (p. 288).

The middle category, termed "the unskilled," included individuals with Down syndrome who were able to perform simple skills under constant supervision. Rosenzweig explained, "These mongoloids have the ability to acquire marketable skills and can be habituated to act in such a manner that pseudosocial competence can be maintained" (p. 288).

The highest category of Down syndrome, termed "the semi-skilled," included people who could successfully learn to perform low-level remedial tasks with limited supervision. Rosenzweig noted, "They possess those added qualities that enable them to rise above their intellectual level" (p. 288). According to Rosenzweig, institutionalization was required for the dependents and the unskilled. However, he felt the semi-skilled could benefit from specialized schooling in segregated classrooms and might be of some use to the wider community.

Etiology Confirmed

While educators, physicians, and parents debated the value of schooling for people with Down syndrome, speculation over the disability's etiology ended. Down (1887/1990) had propagated a belief that tuberculosis in the mother resulted in degeneracy. Benda (1949) had hypothesized that Down syndrome resulted from "a deceleration of the developmental rate due to noxious agents interfering with proper blood supply and nutrition of the growing fetus" (p. viii).

In 1959, using cytogenic techniques developed earlier in the decade, Lejeune, Gautier, and Turpin (1959) discovered the existence of the third 21st chromosome resulting in 47 chromosomes rather than the ordinary 46. This discovery ended the debate on the origin of Down syndrome, but speculation about degeneration and the use of the term *mongoloid* persisted. Merton (1968), for instance, maintained that people with Down syndrome were a direct connection to the evolutionary past. He sought to substantiate his claims by presenting photographs of toddlers with Down syndrome alongside photos of orangutans. He felt the similarities served as proof that chromosomal anomalies resulted from degeneration (forgetting, perhaps, that all toddlers share a resemblance to monkeys).

At a 1967 symposium in honor of the hundredth anniversary of Down's original essay, top researchers on the topic of Down syndrome from around the world discussed at length medical dilemmas shared by people with Down syndrome and orangutans (specifically, postnatal tuberosities in the cerebellum) without once reinterpreting the degenerationist assumptions underlying the conversation (Booth, 1985). Also at this symposium, these same researchers defended the continued use of the term *mongolism*. Only one participant, a Japanese scientist, expressed offense at the continued use of the racially motivated label (Booth, 1985).

THE BIRTH OF ADVOCACY

At the midpoint of the twentieth century and continuing into its latter half, a number of contesting representations of Down syndrome and their consequential treatments once again met in struggle over school identity. Several researchers maintained educational hopelessness as a central feature of trisonomy 21 (e.g., Gibson, 1978; Illingsworth, 1974). However, educability, the potential to learn, was gaining limited recognition in the interpretation of Down syndrome (J. N. Buck, 1955; Butterfield, 1961; Sarason & Doris, 1979). Both Buck (1955) and Butterfield (1961) published accounts of individuals with Down syndrome who demonstrated competencies beyond what was generally believed possible. The researchers then generalized from these case studies to suggest the entire category of Down syndrome might require psychological and educational reinterpretation.

Buck, a psychologist at a state institution, described his first meeting with Benjamin Bolt, then a 42-year-old man with Down syndrome. On the death of his parents, Bolt was immediately incarcerated in the institution. Buck (1955) explained:

> When Mr. Bolt entered my office for his first interview, I glanced up from the papers on which I was working and commented quickly to myself, "Well, well, another Mongoloid imbecile; this shouldn't take long." In appearance Mr. Bolt was patently a Mongoloid, and about as defective a Mongoloid as one could expect to find locomoting without active assistance. (p. 456)

However, beginning with Bolt's "courtly acknowledgement" of Buck's greeting, it became clear to the psychologist that "here was no ordinary Mongoloid" (p. 456). Bolt's tested intelligence quotient on entering the institution was 111. Based on the friendship that developed over the course of several years, Buck concluded that Bolt should serve as a lesson to the field of psychology: "Before too long it may well be demonstrated that Mongolism need not inevitably be accompanied by mental retardation, much less mental deficiency" (p. 456).

Butterfield drew similar conclusions after meeting a young man with Down syndrome who, like Bolt, demonstrated intellectual competencies that exceeded Butterfield's professional expectations. Butterfield (1961) postulated:

> If a single case is unusual enough it can cause one to consider revising concepts which he has regarded as well established and upon which he has regularly based decisions which radically effect the lives of others. (p. 444)

The decisions to which Butterfield referred included the automatic alienation of people with Down syndrome from educational opportunities and their banishment from the community.

Two dimensions of both Buck's and Butterfield's case studies are significant to the understanding of treatment and disability. First, each subject was brought up and maintained as a central member of the immediate family and was expected to participate in the general functions of the household. High expectations had been a part of each of their lives. Butterfield's subject, for instance, had controlled the household budget for years. Second, on the death of each subject's parents, the only community option available for the two men was the institution. Through the 1960s, institutionalization as the eventual destination, if not the immediate response, for individuals with disabilities remained the cultural rule (Blatt, 1987).

However, a shift in sensibilities was occurring. The parents' movement following World War II sought limited community acceptance for individuals with severe disabilities. This was a rudimentary, early form of advocacy constrained by the polite rhetoric of benevolence. In the 1960s, inspired by the growing civil rights movement, particular disability professionals (Blatt & Kaplan, 1966; Dybwad, 1964) joined with parents in a concerted advocacy movement focused not on partial acceptance but on the right of people with disabilities to community membership.

The disability advocates exposed the horrific conditions maintained in state institutions (Blatt & Kaplan, 1966) and worked to develop community-based living options that would bring people with disabilities to their rightful spot as full members of society (Blatt, Biklen, & Bogdan, 1977). Disability rights attorneys began to formulate a legal framework which recognized that a disability did not void an individual's right to protections guaranteed by the Constitution, including the Fourteenth Amendment, which states, in part:

> No state shall make or enforce any law which shall abridge the privileges or immunities of citizens of the United States; nor shall any state deprive any person of life, liberty, or property, without due process of law; nor deny to any person within its jurisdiction the equal protection of the laws. (Section 1)

In response to forced institutionalization, attorneys borrowed a concept from business law, the least restrictive alternative, and renamed it the principle of the "least restrictive environment." The argument followed that in carrying out a state interest, whether that be regulation of commerce or provision of treatment to people with disabilities, the state must impose its agenda in a manner least likely to intrude on individual liberties (D. Biklen, 1983).

Among many victories (including an antidiscrimination clause and an affirmative action clause attached to the federal Rehabilitation Act of 1973), the disability rights movement instigated a profound societal shift toward recognizing the right to an education for all people with disabilities. Litigation in the early 1970s (e.g., *Pennsylvania Association for Retarded Citizens v. Commonwealth of Pennsylvania*, 1972; *Mills v. D.C. Board of Education*, 1972) ruled in favor of schooling for children with disabilities, and led to the passage of a major federal law in 1975, the Education for All Handicapped Children Act (Public Law 94-142, reauthorized in 1990 and 1997 as the Individuals with Disabilities Education Act). This law mandated that children with disabilities receive a free and appropriate public education and that it take place in the least restrictive environment.

THE MAINTENANCE OF THE ALIEN AND THE EMERGENCE OF THE SQUATTER: DOWN SYNDROME IN THE AGE OF ADVOCACY

The 1970s were generally characterized by fairly positive portrayals of the effects of schooling on the development of students with disabilities (Blatt et al., 1977). However, despite an accumulation of data that would suggest otherwise, educational hopelessness continued to be associated with Down syndrome in certain influential segments of the disability sciences (for a thoughtful critique of hopelessness in the 1970s, see Rynders, Spiker, & Horrobin, 1978).

A 1975 article in *Psychology Today*, for instance, suggested that the inclusion of students with Down syndrome in the movement toward public education for all children with disabilities represented a naive and nonsensical waste of public resources. One presumed expert on Down syndrome was quoted in the article as saying, "You show me just one mongoloid that has an educable IQ. . . . I've never seen even one in my experience with over 800 mongols" (Restak, 1975, p. 92).

In an influential 1970s text on Down syndrome, subtitled *The Psychology of Mongolism*, Gibson (1978) echoed the hopelessness of the *Psychology Today* article. He maintained that "inherent limitations of intellectual growth" (p. 33) precluded the ability to reason and suggested that schooling would have little impact on children with Down syndrome: "The influence of nurture is not convincing on the basis of past research" (p. 34).

Despite the educational hopelessness found in much of the 1970s professional Down syndrome literature, the Education for All Handicapped Children Act effectively shifted the struggle for representation for people with Down syndrome from locations of outright banishment to the school. Those who took a dim view of the community potential of children with

Down syndrome were forced to acknowledge that public schools played an increasingly prominent role in children's lives. They argued strongly and successfully, however, for the retention of segregated classrooms for severe and trainable mentally retarded students, categories thought to encompass the intellectual capacities of most, if not all, children with Down syndrome (e.g., Gibson, 1978; MacMillan, 1982).

Strict segregation of children with Down syndrome and others considered to be mentally retarded remains the predominant educational practice in today's schools. In a 1995 report issued by the ARC on the percentage of students labeled mentally retarded sharing classrooms with nondisabled students, only Vermont and Massachusetts exceeded 50%. Eight states and the District of Columbia served less than 1% of their children labeled mentally retarded in inclusive classrooms. The lowest ranking state was Iowa, at 0.3% (ARC, 1995).

Beginning in the 1970s, however, a group of educators grew increasingly organized in their questioning of the educational hopelessness attached to Down syndrome (D. Lane & Stratford, 1985; Rynders & Horrobin, 1975; Rynders et al., 1978). In a response to the 1975 *Psychology Today* article that summarily dismissed the potential to learn for students with Down syndrome (described above), Rynders and colleagues (1978) examined 105 studies yielding data that suggested large numbers of children with Down syndrome had the potential to benefit from schooling in academic content areas. Several later studies established a solid understanding of the potential to learn and reason on the part of students with Down syndrome (Buckley, 1985; Buckley & Wood, 1983; Pieterse & Treloar, 1981, cited in D. Lane & Stratford, 1987; Rynders & Horrobin, 1980; Stratford & Metcalfe, 1982). These studies described in detail the development of reading comprehension and writing skills, computational skills, perceptual recall skills, problem-solving abilities, and other cognitive dimensions considered important in the pursuit of content-area knowledge.

The groundbreaking work of these researchers was considered justification for allowing at least certain students with Down syndrome into "educable mentally retarded classrooms" where limited opportunity to engage in academic content existed. At the same time, a movement was growing in support of *regular* class placement for children with disabilities.

In 1968, Dunn, based on the work of others (Blatt, 1956, 1960, 1966; Dybwad, 1964; Sarason, 1959; Sarason, Davidson, & Blatt, 1962), questioned the efficacy of educable mentally retarded classrooms for children labeled as mildly retarded. Recognizing the continued cultural biases that existed as the basis for such classrooms, Dunn (1968) suggested that regular class placement was a more appropriate and viable option. In 1977, the Center on Human Policy at Syracuse University, emerging as a focal point in the disability advocacy movement, distributed Douglas Biklen's (1977) *The Elementary School Administrator's Practical Guide to Mainstreaming*. The effort to end public school separation of students with disabilities was gaining strength (D. Biklen, 1985; Blatt et al., 1977; Knoblock, 1978, 1982).

In the 1980s, the mainstreaming movement, which led to the call for the inclusion of all children in regular educational routines and contexts, embraced, in part, students with Down syndrome (Booth, 1985; D. Lane & Stratford, 1985, 1987; Perske, 1987; Rynders, 1987). Arguments advancing regular class placement of students with Down syndrome stemmed from two contesting representations. The first, which relied on the discourse of variability, suggested that inclusion be an option for those students who performed academically in a manner similar to that of their nondisabled peers. The second, contrasting argument, based on the disability advocacy call for social justice based on human reciprocity, suggested that no student should be left out of the wider school community.

Rynders and Horrobin, in their variability argument for the "upgrading of educational expectations" for students with Down syndrome, noted that certain children who could prove intellectual competence belonged in regular classrooms. The researchers did maintain a need for segregated options for less advanced children. Rynders and Horrobin (1990) stated:

> It is not our desire to contend that a trainable placement is never appropriate. To the contrary, some children (but far fewer than once thought) will prosper in a trainable class placement because of their cognitive and adaptive behavior impairments. (p. 82)

According to this interpretation, students who, with minimal support, conformed to traditional school standards of individual utility had a heretofore unrecognized right to wider community resources—seemingly self-evident, but a radical idea when first presented. However, it was argued that those children who faced serious conformity dilemmas were justifiably segregated for their own good and the good of the school community.

Booth took a different position in his support of mainstreaming students with Down syndrome. Rather than interpreting inclusion as a privilege earned through demonstrations of norm-based competence, he suggested that participation in nonsegregated settings was a student's right. In his pioneering review of the cultural representation of Down syndrome, Booth (1985) claimed the school context itself could be altered to support all children's membership in the classroom community. He noted:

> Examples of the abolition of segregation by low ability in any systematic way remain rare, although sufficient examples of integration of pupils with a wide

range of disabilities testify to the possibility of including such children within ordinary schools, irrespective of the severity of their handicap, given the appropriate planning and provision. A careful reallocation of resources would enable almost all children currently within schools for those with moderate or severe learning difficulties to attend an ordinary school. (p. 20)

Arguments such as Booth's in support of inclusion for all students were described as a "perceptual revolution" (Perske, 1987, p. 276) in the understanding of Down syndrome. However, the deficit model of impairment attached to trisonomy 21 was firmly maintained. It might be more appropriate to describe this as a perceptual revolution in the location of special education services—again, a radical idea for the time. Mainstreaming children with Down syndrome meant that, based on human rights, educational space would be provided in regular settings but must take on the appearance of the technology of special education to address the unique needs of presumably deficient learners.

Relegating learning differences to the status of impairments that require, even in regular classrooms, the care of professionals specifically trained in special education technology was a theme that ran through the language of PL 94-142, the 1975 law on which inclusion as a legal obligation was based. In section 612, Congress insisted that there be

procedures to assure that to the maximum extent appropriate, handicapped children, including children in public or private institutions or other care facilities, are educated with children who are not handicapped.

At the same time, as pointed out by Rhodes (1995):

The metaphor of illness (e.g., diagnosis, treatment, clinical organization features) was codified and imported directly into the school system by the authority of PL 94-142. . . . The imported medical metaphor of illness constructed differences in learning style as "pathology," "handicaps," and "deficiencies." . . . At one level, the intent of this Act was to insist that public schools include all children without exception. However, the law itself assumed that the ideology of pathology was the only way to read the reality of the lives of children with disabilities. (p. 459)

The law, in effect, codified the four assumptions of special education outlined in Chapter 1: (1) Disability is a scientifically diagnosed condition; (2) identifying disability has educational relevance; (3) special education applies scientific principles unique to remediating disabilities; and (4) progress in special education results from refining disability assessments and interventions.

A common consequence of inclusion based on PL 94-142 was the emergence of the squatter. Within this representation, a set of procedures specific to the industry of special education (e.g., disability assessments, labeling, individual education plans, behavior modification techniques, and functional and readiness curricula) followed children with disabilities as they entered regular environments. In effect, a new border was created between children described as impaired and presumed to require the technology of special education, and those who participated as normal members of the regular classroom.

My use of the term *squatter* has connotations of reduced value. However, I cannot overemphasize that efforts directed toward inclusion in the 1980s were profoundly important to the advancement of citizenship for all students. Not so many years ago, I might well have represented the squatter's position as the educational ideal for students with disabilities. The squatter characterization emerged in my research only after I noted that not all of today's inclusion efforts stalled at the periphery of the regular classroom, just short of the privileged status of citizen (see Chapter 4).

CONCLUDING THOUGHTS ON BANISHMENT

No matter what type of psychological or benevolent justification is currently presented in support of the status of the alien or squatter, relegating students with Down syndrome to the netherworld of the school and classroom is a social artifact of community banishment—the historical sentence imposed through various forms of confinement on culturally devalued groups.

The utilitarian label of "burden," with its consequential segregation, has been applied to all sorts of different categories of people for a variety of reasons throughout time. The single point of commonality among the banished categories has been a general nonconformity to whatever standards happened to momentarily (and situationally) represent the utilitarian model of contributing citizen. If you did not look normal (e. g., if you happened to be other than white, male, and land-owning), and if your potential to look normal was in doubt (e.g., if you were female or you had a chromosomal anomaly), then you were systematically, organizationally, educationally, and culturally excluded from some or all community opportunities.

The Analogy of Home Economics to Special Education

Girls and women have historically suffered educational oppression and school segregation in a manner similar to the treatment of students with

Down syndrome. Walkerdine (1990) offered examples of the devaluation of girls in school as "proof of the existence of the Other, girls' performance as difference, is a constant reassertion that 'woman' exists in her difference from and therefore deficiency in contrast to those rational powers of the mind that are a constituent of 'man'" (p. 62). Just as the performance mannerisms of students with Down syndrome are separated from images of competence, "the concepts of women and knowledge—socially legitimated knowledge—had been constructed in opposition to each other" (Harding, 1986, p. 106).

The imagery of female as deficient led in the early part of the twentieth century to the overt exclusion of girls from academic and community opportunities open to boys. As more and more girls entered and remained in formal public education, home economics emerged as the singularly appropriate educational path for young women to follow in school (Hansot, 1993). It was assumed that girls would naturally become homemakers and child-care providers and that their educational curriculum should prepare them for their future role. As girls progressed through their education to assume the roles of homemaker and care provider, the logic of curricular segregation was reified, or made real.

In an arguably less overt fashion, school devaluation of girls has persisted to the end of the twentieth century. For instance, several studies suggest that teachers attribute boys' skills in math classes to intellect and problem-solving ability, while attributing girls' skills to less valued human dimensions such as following directions and obeying rules (Walkerdine, 1990). Walkerdine (1990) noted:

> In spite of many obvious successes (in math), girls' performance is constantly demonstrated to be different from, other than that of boys. Its very difference, and the constitution of that difference as in some way a deficiency, surfaces time after time. (p. 62)

Entrenched images of educational inabilities associated with girls continue to have an impact on particular academic opportunities important to certain postschool successes. Discriminatory attitudes at school based on what are socially considered to be natural limitations may reduce girls' future opportunities when, in actuality, the limitations are culturally and curricularly determined.

The emergence of home economics as a separate school location singularly appropriate to girls' potential and the continued covert devaluation of female students today is similar to the rise and perpetuation of exclusionary school practices for girls and boys with disabilities. Segregated classrooms were created as a "subsystem of the school community set aside for differences, for separateness, for children treated as other than our-selves. They are outsiders" (Rhodes, 1995, p. 459). The students in segre-gated classrooms for children with disabilities are caught in a system that emphasizes particular differences as deficiencies and routes certain chil-dren in directions that ultimately reduce individual value and community opportunities.

3

The Alien, the Squatter, and the Dilemma of Conformity

Chris Burke, born with Down syndrome in 1965, has become a popular actor in television movies, commercials, and the long-running network series "Life Goes On." He also acts as a spokesperson for the National Down Syndrome Congress and National Down Syndrome Society. The prognosis for Chris at his birth, however, was not optimistic. Doctors told Chris's mother, "Institutionalize him. Forget you ever had him. It will be the best thing for you and your family" (Burke & McDaniel, 1991, p. 41). The doctors advised that Chris be placed in Willowbrook, a Staten Island institution for the mentally retarded.

Had Chris Burke's family not resisted the doctors' advice, he would have found himself in a location akin to hell. Willowbrook was a site of utter hopelessness. Michael Wilkins, a doctor fired from Willowbrook for his efforts to reform the institution, told a media reporter, "In my building there are 60 retarded kids, with only one attendant to take care of them. Most are naked and they lie in their own shit" (quoted in Rothman & Rothman, 1984, p. 16). Parents who visited their children at the institution commonly came upon the most horrific abuse: youngsters with deep bites covering their bodies, dried blood coloring the rags they wore as clothes, bruises, welts, abrasions, and, literally, missing eyes—gouged from the sockets in fits of self-abuse or at the hands of fellow inmates (Rothman & Rothman, 1984).

Because his family had access to resources and support, Chris escaped the sentence of institutionalization commonly imposed at the time on children born with Down syndrome. Not everyone with Down syndrome, however, could similarly escape. Goode (1992), for instance, describes his friendship with Bobby, a 50-year-old man with Down syndrome who had lived most of his adult life in a variety of state institutions. Bobby's clinical records documented a "mental age of 2.8 years. . . . Speech/language therapy is not recommended as prognosis is poor . . . client cannot express complex ideas and understands very little" (Goode, 1992, p. 200). Goode, however, quickly saw beyond the file's deficit-based description. He came to recognize complex and sophisticated thoughts in Bobby's seemingly unintelligible speech. Goode notes that after one instance in which Bobby argued with the institution staff and researchers over the issue of privacy:

> We began to appreciate that cognitively Bobby was far more complex than we had supposed. His appreciation of abstractions such as privacy, as both a local and larger cultural issue, and his 50 years of experience distinguished Bobby's perception of the world from that of a three-year-old. (p. 205)

Goode soon realized that Bobby's perceived incompetence was culturally constructed by those around him: "We heard how our participation with him determined his competence. How we defined Bobby's participation, as in our abilities to understand his utterances, structured his potential competence" (p. 205).

How could Bobby have been shuffled from one treatment facility to the next for nearly 50 years and yet have no one recognize the level of competence Goode discovered in a matter of weeks? The answer lies in the hopelessness surrounding Down syndrome that nearly banished Chris Burke to the horrors of Willowbrook and that still continues to justify keeping certain children with Down syndrome from educational opportunities afforded nondisabled students.

As described in Chapter 2, Down syndrome was first identified as one category of evolutionary degeneracy at the onset of the age of eugenics. It was thought to reflect an atavistic throwback to a brutish and unenlightened age. Though labels evolve, Down syndrome has maintained a prominent position in the categorical representation of cognitive incompetence—the most ugly of designations when one's social value is, in large part, based on perceptions of intellect. The result has been continued community banishment and, more specifically, school segregation as aliens and squatters. In this chapter, I describe the association between students with Down syndrome and mental retardation, their current status as aliens and squatters, and the dilemma children with Down syndrome face in conforming to school standards that define *the good student*.

THE MODEL OF MENTAL RETARDATION: DOWN SYNDROME AND ITS SYMBOLIC STATUS

As practiced today, school and classroom segregation for students with Down syndrome is based on the children's lack of conformity to standards that form the educational parameters of intellectual normality. Students with Down syndrome walk, run, and talk in a manner that falls outside the school's cultural bounds of competence; they often respond to written tests, workbook pages, and assignments in a manner associated with incompetence; they sometimes drool and stick out their tongues, creating an image of incompetence; their phenotype, the manner in which trisomy 21 presents itself physically (as in facial characteristics), is closely tied to images of incompetence. In turn, students with Down syndrome are commonly labeled mentally retarded, "that most despised of the disabilities" (Gwin, 1994: 33), a label that emerged from the medical, psychological, and educational establishments as a metaphor for universal incompetence and that has been accepted culturally as a clinical reality (Biklen, 1993; see below).

The Commutative Law of Down Syndrome

Down syndrome is so closely aligned to the construct of mental retardation that Shayne Robbins, a teacher at Shoshone School involved in my 2-year study, suggested it has come to serve as the cultural model on which our image of intellectual deficiency is based. She explained, "This society has created mental retardation to look like Down syndrome. The way we expect a person to be mentally retarded is the way a person with Down syndrome is. They're poster children." Shayne essentially describes a commutative law of Down syndrome: If MR = DS, then DS = MR, suggesting that it is exceedingly difficult if not impossible for a child with trisonomy 21 to slip the cultural bonds of mental retardation and its consequential social treatment.

Shayne's law is well represented in the professional disability literature. Introductory special education textbooks firmly locate Down syndrome in what is apparently an essential chapter on characteristics of mental retardation (Hallahan & Kauffman, 1997; Hardman, Drew, & Egan, 1996; Heward, 1996). One text notes, "The degree of retardation varies widely among people with Down syndrome; most individuals fall in the moderate range. In recent years, more children with Down syndrome have achieved IQ scores in the mildly retarded range, presumably because of intensive preschool programming" (Hallahan & Kauffman, 1997, p. 130). The possibility of being anything but mentally retarded is never considered. Confirming its commutative aspect, certain of these texts introduce the *mental retardation* chapter with full-page photos of students with Down syndrome engaged in various school activities (Hardman et al., 1996; N. Hunt & Marshall, 1994) or with quotes that suggest mental retardation "conjures up the image of a Down's syndrome individual" (Patton & Payne, 1989: 112).

A brief look at research that involves participants with Down syndrome reinforces the commutative law. We learn that "Down syndrome is the most common genetic cause of serious intellectual disability" (Irwin, 1991, p. 128); that "the defining characteristic of this condition is moderate to severe mental retardation" (Ohr & Fagen, 1991, p. 151); and that "retarded mental development is found almost universally" (Fishler & Koch, 1991, p. 345).

In family-oriented books on Down syndrome, we are told that "parents and members of advocacy organizations are anxious to have the child receive the 'highest' placement in a school setting and therefore *campaign* for the educable [mental retardation] label" (Tingey, 1988, p. 149; emphasis added) as opposed to the trainable label. Parents are advised that mental retardation labels are inevitable but ultimately represent simple necessities for classification; parents, we are informed, should not be concerned about semantics because "it is not likely that a *mere* label will influence children's abilities to learn" (Tingey, 1988, p. 150; emphasis added).

In fact, to suggest that a particular student with Down syndrome is anything but mentally retarded nearly always causes controversy. Recall my own professional resistance to the suggestion made by Melissa's mother that her daughter be allowed to read in school (Chapter 1). In a similar vein, a news bulletin appeared in *Exceptional Parent* magazine that described a film about a child with Down syndrome ("What's Happening," 1993). The brief item suggested the child had *learning disabilities*. In response, an irate member of the Learning Disabilities Association of America demanded that *Exceptional Parent* editors be more sensitive to the learning-disabled population by clarifying that Down syndrome is actually a form of mental retardation, not a learning disability (P.F., 1993; it is the magazine's policy not to print the names of letter writers, though the name came out in subsequent issues).

While admitting she knew nothing about the child or film in question, P.F. (1993) stated, "To equate learning disabilities with retardation is to do damage to a generation of hard-fought and hard-won initiatives of the Learning Disabilities Association and parent-members like myself" (p. 6). The damage done, of course, was the cultural reduction in value of particular learning-disabled students by assigning them the stigma of Down syndrome. Incredibly, editors of *Exceptional Parent* responded by thanking P.F. "for an important correction!" (Editor's Note, 1993, p. 6; exclamation point in original).

In an early and radical analysis of the commutative law of Down syndrome, Sarason and Doris (1979) suggested it was nearly impossible for people with Down syndrome to shed the stigma of mental retardation— their *oddness* in appearance precluded cultural acceptance. Sarason and

Doris's observation was based on the experiences of a young woman with Down syndrome who demonstrated sophisticated thinking and literacy abilities but remained labeled retarded and under the control of various service agencies. Goffman (1963), a sociologist who exerted great influence on our understanding of the cultural construction of deviance, described how those among us who fail to conform to standards of appearance, behavior, and/or communication have what he termed *spoiled identities*, a socially construed *condition* that results in a community position of low value and status. Though we all stray from norms at various times, most of us have developed acceptable means for "managing," or hiding, our transgressions. Students with Down syndrome have no such means. Their appearance and mannerisms are a cultural banner announcing what is believed to be intellectual impairment.

The Consequences of the Commutative Law of Down Syndrome

Down syndrome symbolizes inherent defectiveness. Shayne Robbins expressed this (in critical fashion) in her commutative law, and it was noted in Chapter 1 when Mavis Sherrill described Vic and Greg as "mongoloid"— the reason her neighbor's grandson would not attend East Ridge School. This symbolism consistently emerged over the course of my research. For example, I saw it arise in my observations of a combined grade 5–6 classroom segregated for students labeled as having learning disabilities. Mark Jersey, a 10-year-old with Down syndrome, was one of 12 students in the class. The children had originally been included as members of a nonsegregated, regular 5–6 classroom until a few months prior to my observations, but they had then been segregated into what the excluded students derisively termed "the special ed room." In describing the students' disgust at their fallen status (the emergence of their spoiled identities), Mark's teacher, Jim McClanahan, said:

> The kids in this room are saying, "Like we split, and we're in the special ed room." All the kids in the school are saying that shit, and that's what a lot of the problems are. The kids are saying, "I hate being in the special ed class."

The segregation occurred due to consistent misbehavior by several of the students. Mark, on the other hand, had never been considered a behavior problem; he ended up in the separate classroom because school personnel felt the parents of the other excluded students would be more amenable to the separation if it was justified on the basis of academic needs, not behavioral considerations. As Jim explained it, "We had to tell the parents that we were splitting because of academics. To focus on academics. How are you going to justify an academic split and leave a kid like Mark in the class?" School administrators had feared that parents might question the official, though dishonest, reason for removing the students from the regular class if a child remained who so clearly symbolized academic incompetence.

Mark's separation into the newly formed learning-disabilities classroom created a disturbing situation. Though academically he was one of the better students, his physical appearance, so closely aligned to images of incompetence and special education, made him an alien to this group of angry aliens. Mark's classmates ridiculed him ceaselessly as the symbol of their fallen status. Jim McClanahan said, "He just gets shit on in here, and I was talking to the kids yesterday about it. It's like the pecking order, you know?"—with Mark firmly entrenched at the bottom of the hierarchy.

During one observation, a student near Mark whispered, "Mark, hey, you look at *Playgirl* magazine?" Mark initially ignored the boy, but after several more queries, he gave a shy smile and a nod. The classmate screamed out, "Gross, Mark! You look at naked boys!" Several students began howling, laughing, and shouting, "Stupid!" One boy screamed, "Stupid, man! You are stupid, man!" All Mark could do was cover his head with his hands.

BUILDING THE BORDER: DOWN SYNDROME
AT THE EDUCATIONAL PERIPHERY

Categorical banishment of certain students into special education emerged at the beginning of the twentieth century with the primary and explicit goal of controlling morons. Though the discourse of control has certainly not vanished from justifications for school segregation (see, e.g., Baines, 1997), its primacy has been replaced by a cloak of curricular and instructional considerations that suggest separate learning environments and teaching techniques will assist, at least partially, in ameliorating what are perceived to be educational deficits in children with disabilities (Kauffman, 1995).

Shayne Robbins, from Shoshone School, expressed real shock on returning home from a conference on Down syndrome. There she had encountered workshop after workshop focused on educational goals and instructional practices that were presented as unique and distinct to the needs of children with Down syndrome. She said:

> [Down syndrome] is such a strict community, and there's such a sense that Down syndrome is really, really different—even from other disabilities. When you talk to people who are involved in

Down syndrome—and it's really amazing to me, I went to the
National Down Syndrome Congress, and all of these workshops
that I went to, they would act like it was so exclusive to Down
syndrome.

Shayne disagreed that such a representation reflected the individuality or
human value of any one of the three students with Down syndrome in her
full-inclusion classroom.

Though the logic of absolute confinement apart from the school community eroded with the demise of overt eugenics, entrenched assumptions
regarding the benefits of segregation for students with disabilities clearly
persist. The current manifestation of these assumptions takes the form of
either the alien or the squatter.

Life as a School Alien

Shelly Loveland, first introduced in Chapter 2 as a participant in my study
on schooling and Down syndrome, arrived each morning at her suburban
elementary school, Southwick Lake, on a small, yellow school bus. Only
children with disabilities rode this particular bus. The nondisabled Southwick Lake students arrived at school in long, yellow school buses that
pulled up to the front door.

Shelly's bus parked at a side door, where the children waited strapped
to their seats in what school personnel termed "vests." After a brief period, assistant teachers emerged from the school building and individually unstrapped the students, who were then led or carried to the self-
contained classroom for children with moderate to severe disabilities.

To get to her class, Shelly had to pass by a sign in the hallway listing
the classrooms by grade levels with arrows directing visitors to their building location. At the bottom of the list, with no grade level attached, the sign
read, "Mrs. Lyle's Class." An arrow pointed towards Shelly's room.

Shelly's placement in Josie Lyle's "severe room" (the school staff's
shorthand description for the moderate and severe disabilities classroom)
was justified by the district's special education committee based in part
on her scores on several tests, including the Kaufman Assessment Battery
for Children (Kaufman & Kaufman, 1984) and the Learning Accomplishments Profile–Diagnostic Standardized Assessment (Nehring, Nehring,
Bruni, & Randolph, 1992). These scores suggested that Shelly functioned
at the intellectual level of an 18-month-old child. Shelly's six elementary-
aged classmates in the severe room were said to have mental ages ranging
from 6 months to 4 years.

Josie Lyle, the severe room teacher, however, was skeptical of the assumption that Shelly's ability to conceptualize the world stalled at the level of a toddler. Shelly was nonspeaking, which meant it was extremely difficult for her to communicate ideas and thoughts. At the time of my observations, Josie had introduced the use of an augmentative communication system for Shelly, which allowed expression in a mode other than speech (Kangas & Lloyd, 1988). Shelly was able to gesture to symbols representing requests and to type brief words and phrases on a keyboard (see Chapters 4 & 5). Providing Shelly with an alternative form of communication suggested that she had more to say than her labored sounds allowed.

Still, the severe room served as Shelly's home base, although she had some limited opportunities to join a regular second grade at the opposite end of the school. Her primary segregation was considered essential for the implementation of "diagnostic/prescriptive teaching" (Thomas, 1996, p. 147), an orientation toward instruction distinct to special education. It suggests that students like Shelly have what has come to be defined in medical terminology as *pathological learning defects*. These defects can be *diagnosed* by trained professionals and then remediated to one degree or another through carefully *prescribed* operant learning procedures. Remediation is thought to occur best in structured, segregated classrooms where all children are assumed to share similar learning defects and, hence, similar operant instructional needs; they also have similarly reduced community opportunities (see, e.g., Schopler, Mesibov, & Hearsey, 1995, for a description of the TEACCH system). The logic of diagnostic/prescriptive segregation suggests that "people with retardation who are less mentally competent than the norm cannot aspire to academic and professional choice. A huge chunk of the potential for a higher quality of life has been removed" (Lieberman, 1996, p. 19).

Shelly's severe class curriculum was based on a functional skills model of diagnostic/prescriptive education (Drew, Hardman, & Logan, 1996). The functional goals described in her Individual Education Plan (IEP) included, among others, "Will develop community skills awareness." This awareness was further delineated into subtasks. For instance, one objective of community awareness included, "Shelly will be able to purchase one to two specific items at a grocery store or convenience store independently." When I asked if Shelly was too young to really need grocery store skills, I was told by Shelly's teacher, "If it looks like they have potential in that direction, you really need to get them started early."

Similarly, Mark Jersey partially followed a "functional-based" curriculum in his class. For instance, he spent part of every day working on "money skills," a set of tasks designed to lead to a form of independence in the area of paying bills and making change. His money skills training generally took the form of sitting at a corner table in his classroom sorting change into various configurations of a dollar. He also made a weekly trip to a nearby convenience store where he purchased a small item, generally candy or soda, using appropriate amounts of money and making sure he received the correct change.

The functional skills delineated in the segregated classrooms had little relationship to the general curriculum for nondisabled students. Shelly's brief forays into the regular second grade illustrated this disparity. On one particular day in the severe room, Shelly spent several minutes under the direct guidance of a therapist pushing toy cars to a peer. This was described as a *motor movement* activity designed to incorporate functional physical skills into *naturally occurring* classroom activities. An associate teacher interrupted Shelly's therapy to tell her, "It's time to go to Mrs. O'Mally's room"—the regular second-grade class.

Shelly entered Mrs. O'Malley's classroom while the children read from a text on the importance of family. Mrs. O'Malley wrote the word *important* on a whiteboard using a black marker. Turning back to the class, she asked, "Do you think your family is important?" Several children nodded. One girl raised her hand. Mrs. O'Malley said, "Why do you think a family's important, Tanisha?" Tanisha responded, "'Cause my mom loves me." Mrs. O'Malley wrote the word *love* under *important*. Several other children raised their hands and added to the list of family functions, leading to a general discussion on the community of the family. As the children continued to read and discuss, issues such as food, shelter, and clothing emerged from the topic of family.

On arrival, Shelly took her seat at an empty desk. Following a routine, her neighbor scooted her desk up against Shelly's and laid the text so Shelly could hold half of it. The lesson continued into the next day, when the children, working in pairs, constructed a collage in the shape of a house representing the functions of family. Shelly, who returned for the second part of the lesson, worked with her neighbor on the collage, with Shelly pointing to pictures and her friend clipping them from the magazines. Interestingly, Shelly was quite insistent that a picture of a bathroom be included in the collage. Though her reasoning was unclear, when the students presented their collages, the bathroom scene spurred a discussion on the varied bedtime rituals each child experienced at home.

This transition for Shelly, from pushing toy cars to entering a discussion on family, reflected Josie Lyle's trepidation with the functional curriculum available in the segregated classroom. Josie firmly believed the tasks outlined on Shelly's IEP represented important skills, but she doubted that isolated learning situations in classrooms and environments apart from nondisabled peers could lead to full community membership.

Josie's uneasiness with segregated functional learning had emerged some years earlier in an instructional experience with Matthew, an adolescent student with Down syndrome. Matthew, who was unable to speak, spent his days in an isolated classroom where, Josie explained, much of the curriculum involved connecting plumbing fixtures kept in a bucket in the corner of the room. When the task was completed, the fixtures were disassembled so they could be reattached the next day. According to Josie, Matthew hated the eternal plumbing task; often the fixtures ended up strewn across the room, with Matthew first in a rage and then in time-out. Eventually, Josie reached the conclusion that, "Maybe Matthew doesn't like his job." Her colleagues seemed not to agree. Josie said, "I got looks like, 'What do you mean he doesn't like it? He couldn't possibly have the ability to like or not like because he isn't verbal.'"

Josie likened Matthew's Sisyphean plumbing goal to writing an essay, having it torn up, then being told to write it again: "You'd be out of your head, and I knew then that this was not a nice thing to be doing to people." She felt Matthew needed some escape from the secluded classroom, where throwing plumbing fixtures was just one of his many aggressive behaviors:

> He would grab onto your hair and he wouldn't let go until it was ripped up by the root. Another favorite is he'd get his fingernail in your nostril and twist, and I'd be like, "That is not gentle, Matt. Are these gentle touches?"

Josie interpreted Matthew's behaviors as a demonstration of both social ignorance, stemming from a lack of opportunities to interact with people, and frustration at being kept away from others because of his lack of experience. She said:

> It was like one of those catch-22s where he is aggressive—he likes people so he gets close to them, then he gets too aggressive, but he's aggressive so people don't want to go near him, so they kept him isolated, which didn't teach him anything about going near people.

Noting his school reputation, Josie realized Matthew would never be accepted as a member of a regular classroom, but she did manage to provide limited opportunities for him to interact with nondisabled peers. For instance, she set up a system whereby Matthew was allowed to collect the garbage from each classroom. She admitted, "It's not much, but it got him out of that damn classroom. And he loved it. Then he could wave, and they'd yell, 'Hi!' At least he became worthy of a greeting, and he did, he just loved it."

Josie's discouragement with segregated functional learning was somewhat in contradiction to her position as the teacher in the severe room. Shelly's partial mainstreaming into Mrs. O'Malley's class reflected Josie's intuitive sense of responsibility to reduce, in part, the alienation experienced by students when separated from their community of peers.

Mark Jersey's teacher, Jim McClanahan, expressed similar doubts as to the meaningfulness of Mark's education in the segregated classroom. Jim noted that placement in self-contained school environments ultimately had little to do with a student's *condition*, learning needs, or ultimate goals. Rather, it had much to do with the cultural devaluation of particular groups of people. He explained that when his students were initially separated from the regular classroom (described above), one child with severe disabilities did remain with the nondisabled group:

> It matters if you're rich, if you know how to push the right buttons. Josh remained integrated because his parents knew how to scare the hell out of the people who mattered. They're rich. They got money. They got it, so they kept it. But the other families, well, they bought into what we said because, really, they didn't know how not to.

Jim McClanahan worked hard to open up opportunities for his students to rejoin their nondisabled peers during nonacademic times of the school day, but his efforts succeeded only in creating an inclusive gym class. Jim lamented, "Mark's life stinks. This [segregated class] is a real lousy set up for him. He's like the real perfect kid for an inclusive class."

Life as a School Squatter

In resistance to established school policies that resulted in the creation of segregated learning environments, Jim and Josie exerted tremendous individual effort to seek out limited moments where their students' humanness might be acknowledged and shared by the school community. Both had only limited success. Sporadic, inconsistent, and brief opportunities to join nondisabled children do not result in valued classroom membership, and both Jim McClanahan and Josie Lyle realized this. Schnorr (1990), for instance, followed a child with Down syndrome, Peter, from his segregated classroom into a regular first grade, where he spent brief periods with his nondisabled peers during gym, art, and music. He then returned to his disability classroom for functional learning. Though his trips across the border occurred consistently, Peter was never accepted by peers or teachers as a real member of the class. As one first-grader put it, "He comes here in the morning. He's not in our class. He doesn't ever stay. He comes in the morning when we have seatwork. Then he leaves to go back to his room" (Schnorr, 1990, p. 235).

In response to the continued alienation experienced by students in limited mainstreaming situations, certain educational efforts have been directed toward creating *inclusive* classrooms in which diagnostic/prescriptive instruction is moved from segregated locations to regular classroom sites. This shift in locale acknowledges the alienation from the community inevitably constructed by segregation but maintains a consistent separation of certain learners within the shared environment.

At the East Ridge School, attended by Vic and Greg and a third child who was part of my study, John Frederickson, the tension between images of defectiveness leading to community burden and images of human value leading to community participation resulted in the categorical separation of children within a single classroom. East Ridge had only just begun teaching disabled and nondisabled students together the previous year, and some staff members were upset with the change. One concerned teacher, Sharon Goodall, said:

> You just can't do it. I've been here since this first program started [two decades earlier], and it cannot be done. You cannot take care of those kids [with disabilities] the way they should be taken care of. This school has lost its focus. I mean, integration sounds good on paper, but anything sounds good on paper.

However, Jo Anne Latoya, a colleague of Sharon's (with whom, interestingly, she was co-teaching in the same classroom), held a different view. Jo Anne said:

> A bunch of us—we felt that you're a special ed teacher, and you want to give these kids the least restrictive environment possible, and we're doing the worst thing possible by keeping them in a restrictive environment. This isn't the way!

East Ridge attempted to resolve faculty tension by designing programs that allowed diagnostic/prescriptive operant instruction for particular children while at the same time promoting social interactions among all students. For instance, in Jo Anne and Sharon's class, nondisabled students attended school just three days a week while the children with disabilities, including John Frederickson, came to school five days a week.

On the days that only children with disabilities were in school, Jo Anne and Sharon focused on their students' diagnosed deficiencies. Each of the students with disabilities, according to their IEPs, lacked the ability to pay attention. Jo Anne said that direct instruction in "attending skills" (meaning, "they have to listen to what a teacher says, and teacher directions, and things like that") was a central concern. She explained:

> My first issue is, "learning how to listen." I think that attending, and trying to calm them down in their activity level so that when a direction is given in an activity, or you give them a two-step direction, that they're able to listen to what you're saying, and they're not trying to—like attending, getting their behaviors. You know that when you finally work through listening and attending, you can attack some of the other behaviors like cooperation and playing with friends and those types of things. Even with John [her student with Down syndrome] with his attending problem—there's a lot you can do in the beginning that helps later on. After attending and behaviors, social emotional, then you can start tackling the pre-academics if you want to. Shapes, colors, letters. We have some typicals [nondisabled students] reading!

While the students with disabilities were in school receiving direct instruction in *attending*, their nondisabled classmates participated in neighborhood activities. Jo Anne explained, "Some of them are enrolled in dance group during the day or they do something different. Play groups. Spend time with Mom. It's nice for them, though, because they are only 4. They really don't need to be here every day!" The image of the nondisabled learner benefiting from the community outside the school stood in contrast to the perception that the disabled learners required professional intervention in order that they might someday participate in the community.

On the days when the nondisabled children came to school, the classroom atmosphere radically changed. Jo Anne noted:

> Typicals helped us to see what typical—normal development was like. You see things that you wouldn't normally see. And you see a caring side to children that you usually wouldn't see. . . . It sometimes makes the demands higher for a special needs child that you wouldn't think he could do.

She illustrated the change in atmosphere by describing her new approach to "language group" (a time when her students with and without disabilities joined together for exercises in communication):

I'll start by asking, "Is there anything that you'd like to say? Is there anything that you'd like to talk about? Or anything?" And sometimes my agenda is totally thrown away if there's something someone would like to talk about. Like, "My father was snoring last night and I couldn't sleep." We had that discussion one time probably for an hour and a half. That was classic. It was one of the most classic days. Problem-solving skills, you know, things that you thought normally could not happen during a language lesson. But now they do, and maybe the other kids aren't really saying anything in the conversation, but they can hear it, be part of the process. "What's a conversation all about anyway?" kind of thing.

The limited participation by children with disabilities in the language lesson was based on the assumption that the children's learning deficits inherently precluded active curricular engagement at a level equal in sophistication to that of the nondisabled learners. For instance, John Frederickson, Jo Anne and Sharon's students with Down syndrome, could not speak. The spoken nature of the language lesson inherently prevented his active involvement; his passivity, in turn, was assumed to stem from intellectual deficiencies.

As Jo Anne acknowledged, however, and as observations confirmed, the students with disabilities remained engaged in these groups even when active participation was impossible. It appeared that the *paying attention curriculum*, implemented on segregated days, had less impact on students' developing attending skills than did the act of increasing the complexity of the activities themselves. The level of attention demonstrated by students with disabilities reflected their level of interest in the topic at hand: On days when the nondisabled students joined the class, adult-established functional skills and operant instruction were deemphasized and largely replaced by child-initiated and cooperative activities focused on what teachers described as *developmentally appropriate* learning goals.

Nonetheless, the presumption of learning deficiencies and the manner in which teachers structured activities led to a distinct separation between disabled and nondisabled learners on the days when the two groups joined (and, inherently, on the days when only students with disabilities attended school). I also observed this in several other classrooms that brought operant prescriptive teaching into the nonsegregated classroom. For instance, Joanna Sylvester, a participant in my study, was included along with four other children with disabilities in a regular second grade as a full-time member. At the same time, teachers consistently grouped the five children with disabilities apart from the nondisabled students—often in the hallway, where they were taught separately by an assistant teacher during all academic-content periods of the school day.

DELINEATING DEFECT: DOWN SYNDROME AND
THE DIFFERENCES THAT MATTER

The separation of students with Down syndrome from their nondisabled peers is guided by the principle of utilitarian individualism serving as the functionalist foundation for segregation. Within a utilitarian framework, the school's primary purpose is to demarcate and develop citizens who will contribute to the community through their individual efforts. Schools succeed by efficiently *transmitting* knowledge, which allows certain students to fill valued occupational roles in our complex, technologically driven society. Soltis (1993) explains:

> Students are often put in competition with each other for grades, and cooperative activities are generally shunned. A form of utilitarian or entrepreneurial individualism is encouraged by such practices and teachers as well as students seek more to enhance their self-interest than the interest of the school as a community. (p. 154)

Within this framework, certain students, including those with Down syndrome, stumble. Reflecting functionalist standards, schools are inherently rational and orderly. Therefore, if particular students do not fit into the classroom, they must represent irrational and disorderly elements and must be removed. One might stumble for any number of reasons. However, in school, any form of the *differences that matter* is generally linked to individual cognitive deficits (Dexter, 1964/1994; Skrtic, 1995a). Even the disability category of *behavior disorders* (emotional disturbance), ostensibly distinct from cognitive concerns, is, in practice, linked to "below average IQs" (Hallahan & Kauffman, 1997, p. 211), and "adversely affected educational performance" (Forness & Knitzer, 1992, p. 13).

Curriculum and Conformity

In my observations of classrooms separating children with Down syndrome as aliens or squatters and in my own teaching experiences in such classrooms, two broad conceptualizations of *regular* curricula were obstacles that hindered the participation of students with disabilities. The first, which generally affects elementary-aged and older students, assumes that the knowledge necessary for individual utility exists in the form of an increasingly complex hierarchy of intellectual skills. These skills are psychologically deduced and scientifically segmented into small steps forming the rungs to the ladder of knowledge.

Teachers, as managers of knowledge, are trained to transmit its scope and sequence to students at an appropriate pace. Students, in turn, are required to conform to behaviors associated with understanding the scope and sequence. For instance, they raise their hands and, when called upon, give spoken responses to teacher questions that conform to expectations of correctness; they write essays in legible script that follow the teacher outline in form and content; and they respond to test questions in a manner that conforms to expected responses. The successful student is one whose performance conforms closely to the expectations surrounding the school hierarchy in math, science, reading, language arts, spelling, and social studies skills.

The second curriculum theory observed in practice, often associated with preschool-aged students, also presumes that a child's ultimate utility emerges in a linear sequence of individual development. However, in this model, rather than being passive recipients of skill training, the children are considered active discoverers of important concepts. Teachers are trained to create activities and situations through which children discover concepts in appropriate and age-normed sequence. Again, student success is measured by performance conformity as laid out by *developmentally appropriate guidelines* (e.g., Johnson-Martin, Attermeier, & Hacker, 1990).

The Dilemma of Conformity for Students with Down Syndrome

Demonstrating conformity to a scope and sequence of hierarchically arranged intellectual skills and concepts, whether transmitted to students or discovered by them, proved problematic for children with Down syndrome. The manner in which conformity was measured tended to require particular behavioral and communication patterns not necessarily shared by students with Down syndrome. A gap, then, emerged between the child with Down syndrome and the performance expectations established to demonstrate knowledge acquisition and individual development. This gap appears on intelligence tests; tests of applied cognition; communication assessments; tests of math, reading, and language; play assessments; and general social skills (Canning & Pueschel, 1990; Fowler, Doherty, & Boynton, 1995; Hodapp & Zigler, 1990; Irwin, 1991; Serafica, 1990).

The difficulty children with Down syndrome encounter when attempting to conform to traditional classroom performance expectations is generally explained away through the metaphor of mental retardation. When one consistently performs *as if* he or she is incompetent, whether it be on tests or on the playground, the result is a scientific label of cognitive deficiency referred to as mental retardation: "We cannot see mental retardation. Nor can we hear, smell, or touch it. We infer it" (Bogdan & Taylor, 1994, pp. 7–8). The label symbolizes a chasm between a student's manner of performance and that which is valued by schools.

In the act of clinically judging students with Down syndrome, we tend to forget the inferential and metaphorical nature of the labeling process. *Reification*—literally to make the abstract a material reality—leads us to believe mental retardation has an objective existence:

> This occurs as the term becomes applied to real people; is thought of as describing particular behavior; becomes associated with particular associations and vocations (e.g., the American Association of Mental Retardation); is an official category written into law (e.g., mental retardation appears in the Individuals with Disabilities Education Act); is used in humor (e.g., moron jokes); has institutions and agencies to monitor, serve, and house people so labeled; and is "found" through testing (i.e., intelligence testing). (Kliewer & Biklen, 1996, p. 85)

Those judged to be mentally retarded, however, may not be so quick to accept its reality. Ed Murphy, a state institution survivor with a measured IQ of 49, noted in an interview:

> You judge a person by how they look or how they talk or what the tests show, but you can never really tell what is inside the person. Take a couple of friends of mine. Tommy McCan and P. J. Tommy was a guy who was really nice to be with. You could sit down with him and have a nice conversation and enjoy yourself. He was a mongoloid. The trouble was, people couldn't see beyond that. If he didn't look that way, it would have been different, but there he was, locked into the way other people thought he was. Now P. J. was really something else. I've watched that guy and I can see in his eyes that he is aware. He knows what's going on. He can only crawl and he doesn't talk, but you don't know what's inside. When I was with him and I touched him, I know that he knows. (quoted in Bogdan & Taylor, 1994: 91)

Ed Murphy's insights, despite his presumed IQ of 49, are a powerful critique of the dilemma of conformity confronted by people with disabilities generally and Down syndrome specifically. Every student with Down syndrome who participated in this research had physical and communication differences (often interpreted as problems) that precluded efficient and effective performance in the dance of competence taking place in each of their classrooms.

The Dilemma of Movement. The relationship between a student's motor ability and clinical perceptions of her or his intellect is not a new or radical association. The famed educator Maria Montessori (1949/1967) identified children's hands as "the companion of the mind" and noted:

In my experience, if—for special reasons—a child has been unable to use his hands, his character remains at a low stage in its formation: he is incapable of obedience, has no initiative, and seems lazy and sad. (pp. 150–151)

Children with Down syndrome, who have had each of Montessori's *characteristics* categorically applied to them, face a unique and exaggerated dilemma with physical coordination when compared to nondisabled peers and peers with (presumed) similar intellectual delays who do not have Down syndrome. These delays are evident, for instance, when researchers compare average ages at which children reach certain *motor milestones*: Children with Down syndrome take about twice as long as other children to smile, sit up, stand alone, walk, climb stairs, and ride a trike (Canning & Pueschel, 1990; Fewell, 1991).

The specific delay in motor coordination is also apparent when disability experimentalists construct laboratory situations to test movements of individuals with Down syndrome. For instance, when they are asked to tap targets with their fingers, the motor responses of people with Down syndrome are slower and less consistent than the movements of subjects without Down syndrome (both disabled and nondisabled) (e.g., Elliott, 1985; Frith & Frith, 1974). When the subjects with Down syndrome are asked to quicken their tapping pace, the effort results in increased pressure, which actually slows the tapping (e.g., Frith & Frith, 1974).

Differences in hand movements grow increasingly pronounced when the task involves a sequence of movements (e.g., Anwar & Hermelin, 1979; Elliott, Gray, & Weeks, 1991). Memorizing the sequence is not a problem, but translating the sequence into action is extremely difficult for people with Down syndrome, who struggle to alter the angle of their gestures. In experimental conditions, subjects with Down syndrome also demonstrate difficulty with timing movements to correspond to external stimuli, such as hitting a button when a bell sounds (e.g., Henderson, Morris, & Frith, 1981; LeClair, Pollock, & Elliott, 1993), and with initiating movement when uncertainty is added as a variable, such as when the target is changed without warning (e.g., LeClair et al., 1993). Also, when conditions external to the task are altered without warning, adapting motor movements proves nearly impossible for people with Down syndrome (e.g., Cole, Abbs, & Turner, 1988; Henderson, Morris, & Ray, 1981).

Though certain researchers have conjectured that motor difficulties intensify the perception of intellectual incompetence (Henderson, Illingsworth, & Allen, 1991; Cole, Abbs, & Turner, 1988), each study cited maintained mental retardation as a central feature of Down syndrome. In the contrived context of the laboratory condition, it is difficult to interpret the meaning of movement differences in the everyday lives of students with Down syndrome.

But to move with a lack of coordination does have real consequences on the perception of one's intellect. Classrooms and intelligence tests alike demand dexterity. According to the Kingsley and Levitz autobiographical account of growing up with Down syndrome, neither Jason Kingsley nor Mitchell Levitz demonstrated problems comprehending the regular high school curriculum (Kingsley & Levitz, 1994). Indeed, both consistently made the honor roll. However, Jason admitted he would rather not have Down syndrome due to his many academic "disasters." When asked to elaborate, he explained:

> Well, when I'm in school, I write slowly and when I write fast my writing comes sloppy and people don't understand my writing. . . . When I'm slow I keep behind . . . about my work. . . . If the bell rings from there, what can I do? I just have to do it at home, and I hate that. (pp. 38–39; ellipses in original)

Jason likened his physical struggle with the pace of school to a battle between his mind and body. "Sometimes," he noted, "I put the pencil down and with my two fists try to punch someone in my imagination because the pressure when I'm doing my work. It's hard for me. Looks like war. In my imagination. But I end up doing it. Slowly" (Kingsley & Levitz, 1994, p. 46). Mitchell noted that his awkward movements resulted in a certain level of harassment throughout his schooling. Some classmates teased him and called him a retard. He said, "People who do the teasing don't know that I have feelings. My feelings get hurt." Mitchell said that at times he felt like telling certain peers, "Hey stop it you bastards" (Kingsley & Levitz, 1994, pp. 46, 49).

In my own observations, I noted that specific coordination problems often separated students with Down syndrome from images of intellectual competence. For instance, as a 3-year-old at Shoshone School, Isaac Johnson engaged in a monumental struggle with a book that resulted in a teacher inadvertently dismissing what might otherwise have been interpreted as rather sophisticated literacy skills.

The struggle began when Isaac approached Barb Chandler, one of his teachers, with a new classroom book. Unable to speak, he resorted to hitting her with it. Recognizing his intent, Barb said, "You want to read it? Well, hold on a minute." While Barb turned back to the task at hand, Isaac plopped to the rug, spreading his arms so the large book landed in front of him opened to the first page, but upside down. He leaned forward and stared at the print, which read, "The colorful adventure of the bee who left home one Monday morning and what he found along the way." The only other symbol on the page was a tiny depiction of a symmetrical beehive.

Isaac let out a sigh. He grasped the book on either side, lifted it, and tried to turn it. His arms, however, were spread so wide the broad book rotated only slightly. He tried again, but again it rotated only slightly. He kicked at it out of clear frustration. Then, with great effort, he pulled himself forward. Positioned almost on top of the book, Isaac tilted his head so the words were, in a sense, sideways rather than upside down. He focused on the print for a brief moment, then scraped his hand along the page. The effort, had it succeeded, would have resulted in Isaac flipping to the second page (the opposite direction than a right-side-up book required). However, several pages turned at once, and he kicked at it again. At that point, Barb came over, looked down, and laughed, "Isaac, you have the book upside down. How are you going to read it like that?" Barb smiled in my direction as she scooped Isaac and the book onto her lap. Her question, answered in his drawn-out struggle, was forgotten.

In a different situation, Lee Larson, a 9-year-old with Down syndrome in a second-grade classroom, was completing a workbook page for a language arts lesson. He squeezed his glue bottle but applied too much pressure, resulting in a glob of glue spread across his desk. He looked surprised, then apprehensive, as he glanced toward an assistant teacher helping a classmate nearby. Lee attempted to scoop the puddle of glue back toward the middle of the desk, drenching his fingers as he did. He promptly stuck his hand into his mouth, resulting in an audible expression of distaste that caught the assistant teacher's attention. Looking over she cried out, "That is not to eat!" Several classmates laughed. One wrinkled her nose and said, "Oh gross!" Lee, who did not speak, was unable to explain the situation. Though he had been working diligently on the assignment, his effort resulted only in a drenched worksheet, an angry adult, a bunch of disgusted classmates, and glue dribbling down his chin.

Movement issues clearly affect academic participation and the perceptions of one's intellect. Shayne Robbins at the Shoshone School pointed this out when she held a developmental assessment for preschoolers and asked, "When you ask a kid to remove lids, pull mats, reach objects with sticks, say two words, are you really measuring cognition? They should call it a movement checklist or something." Gesturing, pointing, writing, raising hands, and other types of controlled motion are important performance modalities when one wants to be taken seriously as a student and as a useful human being. When such movements are difficult, children are often interpreted as incompetent, and generally this incompetence is inferred to be due to a low level of intellect.

The Dilemma of Speech. Isaac's and Lee's inability to speak intensified the dilemmas brought about by coordination differences. Speech is central to communicating competence in schools. For all the nondisabled children I observed throughout the course of my research, speech served as their primary method of communication. In fact, if a child's speech did not conform to that of her or his nondisabled peers, it was defined as a difference that mattered, and the child was automatically labeled disabled. Of the ten students with Down syndrome involved in my ethnography, only two were able to speak more than a few understandable words.

Disability researchers unanimously agree that speech delays consistently appear for people with Down syndrome and that these delays exceed those that are expected for people with (presumed) similar cognitive defects (Kumin, 1994; Miller, 1987). In essence, children with Down syndrome understand more than they are able to say. They demonstrate an "asynchrony in language production relative to understanding and other cognitive skills" (Florez, 1992, p. 167).

Several researchers have suggested that the dilemma with speaking exhibited by students with Down syndrome may, in fact, be related to specific motor control issues (Buckley, 1995; Miller, 1987). Henderson and colleagues (1991) contrasted the relatively simple motor act of tapping a plate, which proved highly problematic for people with Down syndrome, to the dramatically more complex physical coordination required to speak: To tap, they explained, requires "innervation of the muscles controlling a simple finger movement" (p. 239). To produce a word, however, is a far more complicated series of movements:

> [Speech] includes the acts of incrementing subglottal air pressure during the exhalation phase of breathing, adduction of the vocal folds by innervation of the muscles controlling the laryngeal cartilages, and control of cyclical activity in the vocal folds. The latter is caused by increasing air pressure against the undersurface of the vocal folds and releasing it once the folds are forced apart by subglottal air pressure. (p. 239)

Dodd (1975) years ago proclaimed that speech difficulties for people with Down syndrome "must be due to a disability in the motor speech act" (p. 306). However, the entrenched presumption remains that whatever speech one has directly reflects the thoughts that are in one's head (as was critically described by Crossley, 1992). Hence a lack of speech is commonly thought to represent a lack of thought.

Lee Larson's second-grade teacher, Colleen Madison, explained how speech problems affect the perceptions of those around students with Down syndrome:

Somebody once told me that when you've got someone who does not communicate, or when you can't understand their communication, what happens is that people around that person kind of stop communicating to him because they're not getting feedback. What happens is you develop this mind-set that they don't understand. So, you start to talk baby-talk, treating them like a baby.

As with movement dilemmas generally, speech problems (which might well be a specific motor issue) led to intensified images of incompetence and served to further separate children with Down syndrome from curricular demands. The nonvolitional lack of conformity experienced by students with Down syndrome, culturally tied to images of intellectual incompetence, resulted in their standing on the wrong side of the border, staring across a chasm into the regular routines and open opportunities of students who did not manifest the differences that mattered.

CONCLUDING THOUGHTS ON DOWN SYNDROME AND THE UTILITARIAN-BASED COMMUNITY

The functional discourse of special education assumes that the very existence of diagnostic/prescriptive instruction, special classrooms, special schools, and functional curricula inherently contradicts any argument suggesting that those removed from the wider community are socially devalued and culturally stranded (for critiques, see Blatt, 1987; Dexter, 1964/ 1994). After all, it is suggested, here exists a benevolent realm, founded on science, absorbing vast sums of public monies, material resources, and professional time and commitment, with little obvious material return to the community (Shapiro, Loeb, Bowermaster, & Toch, 1993).

This is, however, the cost of convenience we are willing to pay to maintain the functional image of the schools—and, by extension, the community—as rational and orderly locations. Here we are taught that conformity to a specific model of individual effort in the direction of individual ends serves generally to further democratic goals. When a student stumbles, the industry of school segregation is there to objectify his or her nonconformity as *disability*, thereby denying the school's complicity in that student's failure, while at the same time providing a bureaucratic and instructional realm in which to confine the child (Skrtic, 1995b).

Supporters of this process contend that the segregated classroom is based on the science of human behavior, has delineated normality through clinical expertise, has created paths that will lead students in a direction of conformity, and has devised quantifiable measurements, such as social validity (Kazdin, 1989), to scientifically assure us that, at some level, *increased* individual utility is, in fact, individually emerging. Some years back, however, Dexter (1964/1994) warned:

> Many with a deep interest in mental defectives are concerned only to make them less defective, less stupid. This is a truism which is so obvious as to "go without saying." But since hardly anybody says it we do not perhaps fully realize its consequences. (p. 153)

The consequences, as outlined by Dexter, include a concerted effort to fit people labeled as defective into devalued roles, if indeed they can fit at all, based on clinical judgments as to their reduced potential to participate in the community and with little regard for the person's own wishes. Shayne Robbins pointed out that her teaching assistant, Anne, a young woman with Down syndrome, was placed in that position by her high school *transition team* with complete disregard for Anne's protest that she did not wish to teach young children. Shayne explained:

> I went to this planning conference on Anne's future, and no one cared that she didn't want to be a classroom aide her whole life. She wants to be a director. She loves movies, and wants to be in the movie business. But no one cares. I mean, you could start in that direction by looking into jobs in a video store, but they didn't want to hear that. They wouldn't even let her be at her own planning meeting. They really dismiss her.

In a devastating critique of the myth of clinical expertise, Douglas Biklen (1992) pointed out that educational placements, labels, instructional methods, and outcome goals had, ultimately, nothing to do with students' supposed *conditions*. Yet these decisions were central in establishing a student's connection with or disconnection from the community. Choices made about children stemmed not from intrinsic characteristics or needs of the child but from contrasting moral orientations, which ultimately asked, "What do we wish our community to look like?" School segregation perpetuates the stratified community—a place where people who embody the differences that matter end up categorically silenced and their experiences wrenched from valued community relationships.

4

Citizenship in School: Reconceptualizing Down Syndrome

In a self-advocacy newsletter begun by and for people with Down syndrome, Mia Peterson described what it was like to be segregated from the educational opportunities afforded her nondisabled peers. She wrote:

> I started to notice that I didn't like the classes I was taking called special education. I had to go through special ed. almost all my life. I wanted to take other classes that interested me. I had never felt so mad, I wanted to cry. (Peterson, 1994, p. 6)

Mia finished school in segregated placements but then returned after graduation to take content-area courses originally denied her. These included, among others, introductory and advanced journalism, as well as child development. Mia has since gone on to co-lead a study on communication skills and people with Down syndrome with Professor Laura Meyers, a linguist at the University of California–Los Angeles (Peterson, 1996).

Jason Kingsley, who with Mitchell Levitz described life growing up with Down syndrome (Kingsley & Levitz, 1994), notes that his valued participation within the community is really a challenge of recognition posed to those who seek to exclude him, but one that ultimately falls heavily on the shoulders of people with disabilities. He states:

> Now we know that people with disabilities can learn and have a full, rich life. The challenge is to erase negative attitudes about people with developmental disabilities, get rid of the stereotypes and break the barriers for people with disabilities. (Kingsley, 1996, p. 6)

Jason ponders, "How do we erase those negative attitudes?" in light of the fact that "people without disabilities are judging us" (Kingsley, 1996, p. 6). Judith A. Snow (1996), a self-advocate in the disability rights movement, decries this judgment, stating:

How absurd to be judged by others at all, especially by those who have never experienced a disability or who are unwillingly providing us with support or who don't listen to the voices we have. (p. 12)

JUDGMENT AND DEMOCRACY

The judgment of which Peterson, Kingsley, and Snow write stems from the moral framework of utilitarian individualism. It assumes that "the individual is prior to society, which comes into existence only through the voluntary contract of individuals trying to maximize their own self interest" (Bellah et al., 1985, p. 143). Community, then, serves the functional purpose of furthering *individual* efforts to accrue cultural capital. Soltis (1993) has referred to this as "entrepreneurial individualism . . . wherein self-indulgence is cultivated and satisfied" (p. 152).

The framework of utilitarianism maintains that *democracy* exists as a bureaucratic arrangement apart from the general population and is charged with the "protection [of individuals] from external threat and provision of the conditions for personal aggrandizement" (Soltis, 1993, p. 151). Those who appear not to make use of these conditions (supposedly open to all), or who appear to lack the potential to accrue privileges, are systematically devalued as less than full citizens—charged as they are with having the differences that matter.

As described in Chapter 1, however, advocates for the reconceptualization of disability—from community burden to valued participant—hold a very different view of the meaning of democracy. They are aligned with John Dewey's (1916) interpretation of citizenship based in the realization of human reciprocity. He argued that democratic processes must not, indeed cannot, be disengaged from those of us who form the community. Democracy, in Dewey's perspective, "is more than a form of government; it is primarily a mode of associated living, of conjoint communicated experience" (1916, p. 93).

Dewey promoted democracy as a way of life in which community both establishes and is derived from each individual's recognition of the value of every other individual. Such realization comes about through the act of communal dialogue, or, using Dewey's (1916) term, conjoint communication. As Freire (1993) emphasized, democracy can only occur when no person's voice is deterministically silenced:

> Dialogue cannot occur . . . between those who deny others the right to speak their word and those whose right to speak has been denied them. Those who have been denied their primordial right to speak their word must first re-

claim this right. . . . Dialogue imposes itself as the way by which [people] achieve significance as human beings. (p. 69)

The movement to merge the education of children with and without disabilities is based on the belief that to enter the dialogue of citizenship does not require spoken, or indeed outspoken, language. Rather, communication is built on one's ability to listen deeply to others. It is an act through which each of our lives comes to be defined by those around us as "precious and irreplaceable" (Snow, 1996, p. 12). Judith Snow (1996) holds that the dialogic of democracy is ultimately a set of values based on respect, humility, and creative listening:

> [Community] requires a willingness to see people as they are—different perhaps in their minds and in their bodies, but not different in their spirits or in their willingness and ability to contribute to the mosaic of society. It requires the "helper" to have the humility to listen for what the person says he or she needs. Also, the "helper" must see that the interaction "helps" both ways. (p. 12)

Humility, Freire (1993) agrees, is central to democracy. "How can I dialogue," Freire asks, "if I always project ignorance onto others and never perceive my own? How can I dialogue if I regard myself as a case apart from others—mere 'its' in whom I cannot recognize other 'I's?" (p. 71)

SCHOOLING AND DEMOCRACY

As Douglas Biklen (1992) has outlined, society itself is hurt when schools act as cultural sorting machines—locations that "justify a competitive ethic that marginalizes certain students or groups of students . . . [that] legitimize discrimination and devaluation on the basis of the dominant society's preferences in matters of ability, gender, ethnicity, and race . . . and [that] endorse an elaborate process of sorting by perceived ability and behavior" (p. 183). Such a model may meet bureaucratic organizational needs (Skrtic, 1995a), but it teaches little about the complexity of community membership and carries with it a tremendous intellectual, emotional, spiritual, and economic cost (Kozol, 1991).

Success in life requires an ability to form relationships with others who make up the web of community. Though many of us have a certain level of control over who we meet and interact with, none of us can come close to claiming complete control. So we must learn to work with others, and this holds true whether we ultimately are destined to lead a multinational computer software firm, inspire a civil rights movement, raise caring children, bag groceries, or chat and feed squirrels with an old man on a park bench. We have got to learn to get along as individuals and as citizens.

Dewey (1899) believed schools must serve as the sites in which children develop both a sense of commitment to one another and a sense of self-direction leading to "the deepest and the best guarantee of a larger society which is worthy, lovely, and harmonious" (pp. 42–43). In Dewey's tradition, Douglas Biklen (1985, 1992, 1993) has also described schools as potential locations of community connectedness. He and fellow educators have substantiated this vision with detailed accounts of actual educational arenas where all students are welcomed, no voice is silenced, and children come to realize their own self-worth through the unconditional acceptance of one another (D. Biklen, 1992; Falvey, 1995; Ryndak & Alper, 1996; Stainback & Stainback, 1996; Villa & Thousand, 1995).

Such acceptance is the aim when children with Down syndrome join their nondisabled peers in classrooms, and many schools and individual teachers have entered into this effort, which seeks and finds community value in all children. This chapter describes citizenship in school for children with Down syndrome. I delineate certain dimensions underlying citizenship and illustrate their occurrence with examples from my own research and other published materials. Then, in the following two chapters, I closely analyze the meaning of school citizenship for students with Down syndrome as it relates to (1) literacy development (Chapter 5), of central importance in experiencing school success (Cunningham & Allington, 1994), and (2) friendship formation (Chapter 6), a possible consequence of being recognized as communally valuable.

Life as a School Citizen

Isaac Johnson, who was first introduced in Chapter 3, certainly found *citizenship* at the age of 4 when he entered Shayne Robbins's classroom at Shoshone School. Shoshone is a parent-run school with a deep organizational commitment to educating children from birth through age 6 as full citizens of the community. Shoshone is located in the heart of a medium-sized eastern industrial city, and its student population reflects the diversity found in the neighborhoods around the school. It is organized into several classrooms, each with 10 to 16 students of multiple ages and ability levels. It is seen by the area school districts as an exemplary program for *all* young children, including those with what are defined as the most severe disabilities.

Isaac, by clinical judgments, might have been considered *low-functioning*. He had no speech that was understandable to teachers; moved with a great deal of awkwardness; had severe dilemmas with fine motor tasks, such as turning pages in a book or grasping objects; and scored poorly on developmental instruments, including the Hawaii Early Learning Profile (Furuno et al., 1988) and the Carolina Curriculum for Preschoolers with Special Needs (Johnson-Martin et al., 1990). For instance, at the age of 52 months, Isaac demonstrated in testing situations a number of skills regarded as appropriate to a toddler's level of cognitive functioning.

Shayne, however, did not see Isaac, or any of her students, as defective. In her classroom, which contained 6 students clinically identified as disabled (3 with Down syndrome, including Isaac) and 10 students considered nondisabled, Shayne and her associates worked to create a context that supported all children's full participation. Shayne explained:

> It's not like they come here to be labeled, or to believe the label. We're all here—kids, teachers, parents, whoever—it's about all of us working together, playing together, being together, and that's what learning is. Don't tell me any of these kids are being set up to fail.

In establishing a representation of citizenship for all, Shayne recognized the transactional relationship of human reciprocity: Community acceptance requires opportunity for individual participation in the group, but opportunity cannot exist outside of community acceptance. As such, Shayne had to foster a sense of the collective that took seriously the value and idiosyncrasies of her individual students. In doing so, Shayne felt that she broadened and strengthened the learning opportunities opened to all her children.

Community built on the recognition of individual value occurred through a curriculum developed by Shayne in dialogue with her students. For instance, her student Isaac was born into a family that loved books. On a visit to his home, his mother told me, "Isaac's surrounded by reading. From Marx to the Bible, it's everywhere he turns!" Shayne agreed:

> You know, I've never met a more literate family in my life. I mean really and truly, Isaac has been part of family reading, Bible reading, his mom has been reading books specifically with him since I started with him, and I know long before that—because that's what she does with kids, and she does it wonderfully.

In the midst of this literate realm, Isaac had developed what Shayne recognized as a love for Maurice Sendak's children's stories, with his favorite being the classic *Where the Wild Things Are* (Sendak, 1961). Shayne's classes in previous years had always emphasized Sendak's books. She based classroom themes around, among others, Max's journey to the land of the Wild Things (Sendak, 1961) and *In the Night's Kitchen* (Sendak, 1970). Many of the projects that emerged from the stories, however, involved fine motor abilities that proved frustrating for Isaac. For instance, the children had made panoramas of the Night's Kitchen using recycled garbage or had constructed bulletin boards depicting personal interpretations of Max's dream through drawings, paintings, and cutting and pasting.

Shayne found these activities to be valuable but wanted to extend them to involve Isaac's strengths, which included a thespian's love for the dramatic. She thought to herself, "What are you going to do? Sit a kid in the middle of things, use a book he loves, and frustrate the hell out of him?" She did not interpret Isaac's broad and impulsive motions, indecipherable chatter, and tendency to interrupt circle time with loud points of exclamation as manifestations of defectiveness. Instead, Shayne saw these behaviors as reflective of Isaac's joy in the drama of life and his desire to connect to his peers. She noted:

> He tells the most amazing stories. I know you've heard him. But he'll just [she made a series of babbling sounds]—like that. And he'll be acting it out, incredibly dramatic, and you'll have absolutely no idea what he's saying. Nothing. Zero. Nothing. There's not one intelligible word in there. But I know him. And I'd say, from knowing him, watching him here, at home, that it's all story-related. The first time I tried reading *Where the Wild Things Are*, which is his favorite book, he couldn't sit. He had to be up, dancing in the middle of the circle, acting it out. He just couldn't resist. He could not help himself. It got all the kids going. We were all Wild Things and it just came alive!

Shayne's ability to listen deeply to the sounds of Isaac's competence struck me in an early visit to the class. Walking through the door decorated with portraits the children had painted of each other, I literally ran into Isaac, who raced in his awkward way across the classroom holding a bottle of lotion above his head. He set the bottle on a shelf, waved his arms wildly, punched his fist into the air, shouted out a long series of sounds, and plopped a baseball cap sideways on his head. He then raced back across the room with two classmates following closely behind.

Shayne, taking note of my confused expression, said, "Isaac, tell Chris about your game." But Isaac and his peers had little time for an ignorant adult as they again raced past me. He shouted a few sounds in my direction and was off. Shayne confirmed Isaac's explanation, saying, "That's right, Isaac. That's your favorite game. At home, that's his favorite game to play with his dad." "What is?" I asked. "Dinosaur-Frontiersman!" she said with feigned exasperation, "Weren't you listening?"

Based on Isaac and his peers' keen interest in stories generally and in Sendak specifically, Shayne proposed an idea to her class. She suggested that the children create and perform a play based on *Where the Wild Things Are.* "This," she explained to the children, "means you write the play, learn the lines, and create scenery, costumes, and props."

The children set out with teacher support to do just that. In groups they dissected the book's text into dialogue and description, then merged each group's ideas into a single script. Children brought in materials to construct costumes and props, and they performed the play for each other. Different roles were shared among students, but Isaac was most excited when he got to star as Max (though he appeared quite pleased with being a Wild Thing as well).

The Wild Thing production was not an add-on to a preexisting curriculum. It reflected Shayne's unique approach to building community through the processes of learning. Within the web of activities, Shayne and her co-workers systematically developed opportunities for their students to engage with literacy and numeracy skills, problem-solving and critical thinking processes, and interpersonal capacities. Though the children may not have been aware of it, learning was always of central concern.

Throughout the classroom activities, Shayne maintained a focus on individual goals for each child. She did not dismiss the linear developmental progression laid out for children by developmental theorists (as translated by educational researchers and publishing companies). She recognized these norm-referenced guides as important for certain students' future acceptance and success as they entered public elementary schools. Shayne explained, "You can get a sense of where a kid is compared to where people think they should be" when using developmental guidelines. She and her co-workers met several times a week before and after school, often until late into the afternoon or evening, discussing each child's classroom experiences and maintaining general portfolios on demonstrated skills and areas of concern. The portfolios included children's work, notes kept by the teachers, assessment information, and narratives written for conferences with parents.

Shayne did not, however, interpret a child's nonconformity to developmental theory as a manifestation of defect. "So what," she continued, "if you don't fit exactly what you're supposed to? You know, it's not like I fit many people's idea of what a teacher's supposed to be like." Shayne recognized a child's nonconformity as natural human diversity; a source of strength that could be supported by the school community in order that it add a unique and valuable dimension to that community. In doing so, developmental theory itself was altered. Rather than existing as a linear progression that falsely split a child's intellect, communication, social presence, emotional presence, and physical abilities into *domains*, norm-based development became a pragmatic set of ideas judged against a child's connection to the community—in effect, judged against democracy: When useful for citizenship, developmental guidelines were used as one way to interpret Isaac and other children's strengths. However, when citizenship was hindered by strict adherence to a monolithic path of progression, developmental guidelines were set aside. For instance, recognizing Isaac's love of reading and his capacity to decipher printed language, an important bridge to the community, required that Shayne see past Isaac's low scores on cognitive developmental checklists, which included numerous references to literacy skills (see Chapter 5).

Shayne also focused attention on one of her classroom associates, Anne, who, as described in Chapter 3, had been left out of her high school transition planning conference. In this meeting, her committee had decided that Anne, who has Down syndrome, would become a preschool aide. Anne did not particularly care for young children and was unhappy with the prospect of spending her life working with them. As Shayne explained, "Anne wants to be a Hollywood director. Period." Shayne realized this desire grew out of Anne's love of movies and so took it upon herself to find a video rental store that would hire Anne. Shayne noted, "At least it's a move in the right direction. I mean, it's not Hollywood, but it's movie-related. That's what she loves, and she knows every movie that's ever been made."

Shayne pointed out the irony experienced when she proposed to the transition committee that Anne's work site be changed to a video store: "They didn't think it was realistic, that she could handle that job. Here they have her educating America's future, but they're scared to let her work at a movie place."

Shayne succeeded in finding a family-owned movie rental shop that hired Anne. Anne quickly learned to work the computer-based rental system under the guidance of the store's other employees; she learned to sort movies, replace them, locate them, and clean the store with the other employees at the end of the work day. Shayne noted, "She's really doing well. People come to her for advice on what movies to get, on what's good, what's current. She knows it all. She's doing really well." Beginning with the simple act of listening, Shayne created not only a valued community role for Anne but one that the young woman relished.

THE ELEMENTS OF CITIZENSHIP

Shayne's efforts with both her associate and students created a context in which traditionally devalued and dismissed individuals found community membership and connection within a framework of academic, social, and community achievement. Doing so required both a reciprocal recognition of each student's inherent value to the community and participatory opportunities that assisted in establishing and confirming that value. Van der Klift and Kunc (1994) describe these two inextricably linked dimensions of citizenship as forming the foundation of a "valuing paradigm" (p. 396). Such a paradigm, they suggest, is a distinct shift away from mere school tolerance of diversity defined by resignation and benevolence. To value another is to recognize diversity as the norm. It establishes the equal worth of all schoolchildren, a sense that we all benefit from each other, and the fundamental right of every student to belong.

In an extensive study of the acceptance and respect accorded severely disabled and nondisabled people, Bogdan and Taylor (1989) noted that these relationships include: (1) the attribution of thinking to one another; (2) the ability to see one another's individuality; (3) the ability to view the relationship as reciprocally valuable; and (4) the attribution of a valued social place for one another. Though Bogdan and Taylor focused on relationships outside of school, these dimensions appear to be critical to establishing a recognition of citizenship for students with Down syndrome in schools, as described below.

A Belief in One's Ability to Think

Schools have traditionally taken a narrow position when defining and judging student intellect (Gardner, 1983). The presence of a thoughtful mind has been linked to patterns of behavioral and communicative conformity associated with competence in logical-mathematical thinking and linguistic skills. Assessments of how well a student conforms to expectations (measurements through which students come to be defined either as smart or as lacking intellect) tend to focus teacher attention on the child's adeptness at responding to classroom-based math and language tasks. These evaluative instruments supposedly measure either a student's understanding of a transmitted knowledge base (hence, a preexisting one) related to math and language, or the student's ability to discover the knowledge base through carefully contrived activities.

Two broad psychological responses have been presented in opposition to the rigidity of school-established intellect. The first suggests that professional reliance on a narrow interpretation of mathematical and linguistic characteristics when defining school citizenship in no way captures the multiplicity of *knowledges* valued in the wider community (Gardner, 1983, 1991, 1993). The second questions the very idea that an objective knowledge base preexists apart from a partial human being (a child) who is then manipulated along a linear instructional path toward what comes to be seen as knowledge (or individual) completion (Vygotsky, 1930–1935/1978).

Broadening the Definition of Valued Intellect. The argument that school learning and community success have, at best, only a weak positive correlation has a long and contentious history (Jungck & Marshall, 1992). Though numerous educators have acknowledged this gap between the schooled mind and the valued citizen, perhaps the most accessible critique is that of Howard Gardner, a psychologist and educational researcher. In describing the *superficiality* often found in school learning, he notes:

> Those students who exhibit the canonical mind are credited with understanding, even when real understanding is limited or absent; many people . . . can pass the test but fail other, perhaps more appropriate or probing measures of understanding. Less happily, many who are capable of exhibiting significant understanding appear deficient, simply because they cannot readily traffic in the commonly accepted coin of the educational realm. (Gardner, 1991, pp. 12–13)

In turning his attention to school-based literacy and mathematics instruction, Gardner points out a peculiar disjointedness between classroom learning and the problem-solving, critical thinking needs of students when they enter the wider community. In terms of mathematics, for instance, Gardner notes:

> Mathematics teachers report that students are nearly always searching for steps to take in solving the problem—"how to plug the numbers into the equation, how to follow the algorithm." The more closely the ordering of words in a problem parallels the order of symbols in the equation, the easier the problem is to solve and the more the students will like it. Seeing mathematics as a way of understanding the world, of illuminating a phenomenon, as a kind of conversation or enterprise into which even a young person can become meaningfully involved is a rare occurrence. And yet, how can genuine understanding ever begin to come about without such an attitude? (Gardner, 1991, p. 165)

Gardner (1991) answers his own question by suggesting, as did Dewey, that schools must first reorganize themselves into locations where the three

R's are posed as "problems, challenges, projects, and opportunities" (p. 187). In this way, students would be required to thoughtfully draw from and apply the skills encompassed in what are traditionally considered the basics of learning.

Second, school personnel, Gardner proposes, must expand their vision of what constitutes valued patterns of learning. In this way, schools would become locations that much more closely mirror what and who are valued in a participatory democracy. Gardner's research to this point has yielded seven such valued patterns for solving problems and fashioning products. Included are the two traditional school emphases on (1) logical-mathematical thinking and (2) linguistic capacities. But Gardner also includes five other culturally valued ways of knowing and acting in the world that are commonly neglected in schools: (3) a spatial-representation intelligence—the capacity to represent the complexity of time, space, objects, and spirit through symbols, drawings, and other media; (4) musical intelligence—the capacity to communicate meaningfully through the creation of song and rhythm; (5) kinesthetic intelligence—the capacity to use one's body to communicate, solve problems, or to make things; (6) interpersonal intelligence—the capacity to deeply understand the communication of others; and (7) intrapersonal intelligence—the capacity to deeply understand one's self, to make choices, and to act on those choices.

Gardner is staunch in his belief that these seven patterns for conceptualizing the world are in no way exhaustive, suggesting that there are probably 10,000 possibilities to be added to the list. He has accumulated cultural evidence that may lead to an eighth addition, that being a naturalist's ability to sense patterns and organization in what on the surface appears to be a chaotic universe (Gardner, 1995). Each intelligence reflects what is currently valued in our culture and thus is socially constructed and historically situated. As culture shifts and time moves on, the *multiple intelligences* described may radically change.

Though Gardner's work might, ultimately, have a utilitarian dimension in establishing human value, he has effectively broadened our interpretation of what it means to be smart. In doing so, he has transformed the school notion of intellect from a rigid, intrinsic commodity to a cultural construction widely shared by individuals traditionally devalued in the educational arena. Hence, he has made it that much harder for segregationists to support their logic of banishment when a child struggles in a rigid curriculum.

Reconceptualizing the Objective Knowledge Base in School. Lev Semenovich Vygotsky was an early-twentieth-century Soviet psychologist whose work is currently experiencing a posthumous popularity. His work is as fundamental as Gardner's in recontextualizing the meaning of intelligence. Although he acknowledged that our ability to understand and act in the world certainly has biological underpinnings, Vygotsky believed that the higher-order thought processes that make us uniquely human exist first and foremost in the social and cultural relationships between a child and the collective. Only after the child has entered into relationships that involve "voluntary attention, logical memory, the formation of concepts, and the development of volition" (Vygotsky, 1981, p. 163) do these culturally crafted, higher-order dimensions establish themselves as attributes of the individual child's psyche. Vygotsky (1981) explained:

> Any function in the child's cultural development appears twice, or on two planes. First it appears on the social plane, and then on the psychological plane. First it appears between people as an interpsychological category, and then within the child as an intrapsychological category. (p. 163)

In Vygotsky's scheme, children are not mere receptacles of knowledge transmitted to them by teachers, nor do they go through biologically determined sets of stages that must emerge in linear fashion prior to acquisition of increasingly complex understanding. Instead, Vygotsky understood children to be active constructors of knowledge who constantly enter into new relationships of understanding with adults, peers, and materials. These new relationships serve to reformulate past understanding, which then reconstitutes the web of relationships, leading, again, to new relationships and continued reformulation and recontextualization of understanding. More advanced members of the cultural collective (such as teachers) serve to facilitate these relationships in a direction valued by the community. At the same time, the child's recontextualized understanding influences the web of relationships such that the culture of the community is itself altered by the active engagement of the child.

In this viewpoint, the manner in which a child conceptualizes the world does not exist first in an objective fashion apart from the child as a rigid boundary within which his or her thoughts must fit. Rather, the mind is forever dynamic, emerging through the multiple relationships formed and re-formed between children and their surroundings. As such, it makes no sense to define any single individual as intellectually defective. The presumed defectiveness exists not as an intrinsic commodity of the child whose thoughts fail to fit within the perceived static border of normality. Rather, the idea of defect emerges from culturally devalued sets of relationships that that child has with his or her surroundings (i.e., teachers, peers, and materials). As Vygotsky (1993) ardently noted:

Why do the higher functions fail to develop in an abnormal child? Not because the defect directly impedes them or makes their appearance impossible. . . . The underdevelopment of the higher functions is a secondary structure on top of the defect. Underdevelopment springs from what we might call the isolation of an abnormal child from his collective. (p. 199)

Vygotsky found that the *culture* of segregation surrounding people with disabilities actually teaches underdevelopment of thinking through the isolation of children from socially valued opportunities. As described in more detail below, altering the culture of disability requires that a child be recognized as an active learner, a thinker, and a problem-solver, but this cannot occur apart from relationships that allow for such engagement.

Believing in a Child's Mind: Renegotiating Down Syndrome and the Ability to Think. Though Shayne Robbins at Shoshone School did not engage in extended discussions of Gardner or Vygotsky, she intuitively rejected the notion that nonconformity to the academic norm meant a student inherently lacked intelligence or was intrinsically burdensome. Instead, she saw incompetence as a perception ascribed to a child by others who misunderstood the meaning of the child's performance. Colleen Madison agreed with Shayne that no child was inherently an intellectual burden to a classroom; in fact, she argued, each student contributed a unique and potentially valuable dimension to the web of relationships that formed a school community.

Colleen served as lead teacher in Lee Larson's second-grade classroom, which included 27 students, 3 of whom were defined as disabled. Lee was introduced in Chapter 3 struggling with his glue bottle. Though incidents like the glue dilemma did at times distance Lee from his peers, he was generally considered a full member of the class. Colleen noted:

If you came into the room and were told there was a retarded child in the class, a child with special needs, I don't think you would pick Lee out. The kids really agree that he's as capable as they are. Intellectually the same.

In light of Lee's distinct facial characteristics associated with trisonomy 21, his awkward body movements, and his inability to speak more than a few understandable words, I was surprised at Colleen's statement. After all, his psychological tests had, at the age of 7, suggested that he functioned at the cognitive level of a 2-year-old, which translates into a severe mental disability. "Wouldn't anyone who comes into the room pick out Lee as the mentally retarded student whether or not that label holds any meaning?" Colleen hesitated at my disbelief, then chose her words carefully:

I suppose you could argue that and it's hard to argue that you might be wrong. Lee is, in a sense, in a way he's branded. People see him. They see Down syndrome. They see mental challenge, retardation, whatever you want to call it. That's what they see, but they wouldn't be seeing him. Do you know what I mean? Because Lee is Lee, and anybody who knows Lee knows, and this includes all the kids, they know he's gifted—in how he solves problems, cares about others, reads, loves math. So I guess what I'm arguing is that if you did pick Lee out, you wouldn't be seeing Lee. It's not Lee you're picking out. It's your stereotype, your mind-set. It's you, and it has nothing to do with Lee. But if that's how you choose to see him, I don't know that anything I could do, we could do, I don't think there's anything Lee could do to change your mind.

According to Colleen, suggesting that Lee's intellect precluded his right to belong simply meant that you were describing a child she did not know. You were proposing the existence of a mythological creature, an illusion constructed in a rigid mind that could not see past the presumption of defect into the smile of a little boy who defiantly demanded a handshake from his teacher at each morning's "greeting time," just like all the other little boys in his second-grade class (the girls split evenly in accepting hand-shakes versus hugs).

Shayne Robbins confronted such an illusion as described by Colleen in a conflict with her school psychologist. In a testing situation, the psychologist asked Shayne's student, Isaac Johnson, to sort spoons and blocks into various containers. Isaac struggled first with the containers to get to the materials. He then separated the blocks from the spoons and tasted from each spoon before throwing them aside, one after the other. He was not given credit by the psychologist, who noted that Isaac had not conformed to the specific directions of the test item. Shayne exploded, "He didn't get credit for it because he didn't do it right, but he clearly knew which was the block, which was the spoon. And he followed directions in an organizing sense."

Shayne knew Isaac: She understood how he organized his experiences and how he related to new and strange environments and unfamiliar adults. She recognized that in his response to the test item, Isaac had, in effect, recontextualized the assessment situation to better fit his movement and speech problems. She explained, "He uses his imagination, he pretends—that's how he makes sense of things. He relates stuff to the books we read, the things he does at home." Isaac's licking of each spoon was an act of imaginative play that allowed him to engage the demands of the psychologist in a manner that conformed to his experiences. The psychologist, who knew little about him, defined Isaac's actions as manifestations of cognitive defect separating the child from the intellectual norm. Shayne, who knew Isaac well, defined his actions as a complex, sophisticated, symbolic response to a difficult situation, one that transformed the context into a more meaningful and thoughtful experience.

A Belief in One's Individuality

Along with recognizing an individual's ability to think, Bogdan and Taylor (1989) suggest that respect and citizenship require a realization of the person's individuality. This is as true in school relationships as it is in our wider community relationships.

In Chapter 1 I described how Mavis Sherrill at the East Ridge School noted that Greg Lafrey and Vic Schroeder served as representatives of the mongoloid category. As such, and despite the seemingly natural inclusion occurring in their class, they were the reason the grandchild of Mavis's neighbor did not attend the school. For some, the boys' uniqueness and individuality were superseded by their association with defectiveness.

School citizenship requires that students not be categorized and separated based on presumed defect. The phenomenon of categorization at the expense of individual value has been described as a "disability spread" in which we

> extrapolate the characteristics we associate with the notion of disability to the particular individuals we meet. These perceptions are often based on stereotypes and what we think we know about a particular disability. They are expressed in predictable ways. For example, "All people with Down syndrome are happy." (Van der Klift & Kunc, 1994, p. 398)

The metaphor of "spread" illustrates the image of defect blanketing the unique humanness of students charged with the differences that matter. What is hidden under the cloak of incompetence is the individuality and personality of the human being.

Teachers who valued their children as citizens recognized each student's individuality. As Shayne Robbins noted when describing her three students with Down syndrome:

> I don't tend to see Down syndrome as something. If you look at those three kids running around the room, they're incredibly different from each other. They're different in terms of what their

bodies are like, how they best communicate, what they're like socially, their interests. And with those three kids in the room it would be hard to say, "This is how you should teach kids with Down syndrome." They are not at all alike.

According to Shayne, the notion of Down syndrome often obscures our ability to recognize the child as a child. She or he becomes a walking pathological syndrome, a mobile defect on the loose. John Mcgough experienced such a disability spread during his high school education in North Hollywood, California, where he attended a segregated school with other students who also had Down syndrome. According to Andrews's (1995) detailed ethnography, John's North Hollywood existence was a lonely and isolated one. Outside of his family, he had few acquaintances and little community connection. His school experience was stagnant and filled with hopelessness. School personnel labeled him "uneducable."

John's life changed dramatically when he and his family moved to Mendocino, California. Beginning with regular trips to the town post office, John began to connect with his neighbors, who appeared able to see past his chromosomal anomaly to his humanity. His relationships expanded from the post office to friendships with a wide array of the town's populace. One of John's siblings noted:

> Mendocino is what John needed—it's what he never had in North Hollywood. It's safe—what he calls a "safe space." Like a lot of people in Mendocino, he's accepted for what he is, not what he isn't. And he can concentrate on what he can do, instead of being shown or being told what he can't do. (quoted in Andrews, 1995, p. 105)

John himself recognized his newfound community acceptance. He explained, "I feel there's a big change coming. It's all good. In a long, long time, I never had such a loving family full of characters like this town family. I may do something different soon" (quoted in Andrews, 1995, p. 106). What John did, in addition to developing an extensive network of friends, was to become a recognized artist. His paintings have been displayed and have sold at a number of shows across the United States.

A Belief in the Reciprocity of the Relationship

Acknowledging students with Down syndrome as thoughtful, creative, and interested learners with personal identities that distinguish them from all other people suggests an individual value that enhances any context containing the child. In classrooms that recognize all children as citizens, teachers and peers have rejected the image of community burden attached to Down syndrome. Rather, the student is recognized as a participating member of the group. Van der Klift and Kunc (1994) note:

> We will not recognize the diverse contributions of those who wear obscuring labels until we move our focus from the disability and look for the complexity and individuality we take for granted in ourselves. Only getting to know a person in all his or her multifaceted individuality can cause the "huge" disability [spread] to magically shrink and assume its real proportion—only one small facet of a person. Only then will we find ourselves able to see and receive the variety and richness of possible gifts. (p. 399)

Shayne Robbins did not hesitate in her response when asked why she devoted so much energy to creating a classroom community where all were afforded citizenship. "Don't think," she told me, "that those special needs kids drain anything. That class would not be half what it is if any one of those kids got segregated. We're all together in there."

As an example, one of Shayne's students with Down syndrome, April Carpenter, played a pivotal role in assisting a classmate who returned to school deaf following a battle with meningitis. Cathy had previously been defined as nondisabled, and then, suddenly, she could not hear. Cathy's classmates had discussed her illness and its consequences, and they had generated ideas for welcoming her back in a supportive manner. April, who did not speak but used extensive signed English, had remained relatively quiet throughout these discussions. However, when Cathy returned, I observed April immediately reach out to her. On Cathy's first day back, April refused to sit at her regular circle time spot; instead, she ignored initial teacher protests and located herself beside Cathy. The two sat together holding hands. Shayne noted:

> Now April, she's really an assertive kid, and one of the things that I've thought has been really neat is her style with Cathy because I think she really—of all the kids maybe two really figured out how to interact with Cathy quickly. April's style in general really helps because she's an in-your-face and signing kid. She's not using her voice to say a lot that Cathy can't understand, and Cathy knows that. But I've also seen April adapt her behavior. She's doing a lot more initiating with Cathy, who isn't doing a lot of initiating with the kids. But Cathy is really into her, and it's really neat because April can be the model now, and that's not something she's been a whole lot. It's wild. They have a great friendship.

April's participation in a classroom that recognized her individual worth and that supported her connection to the wider community had powerful consequences on that community. Shayne saw past April's low developmental assessment scores and recognized in her a deep commitment to her peers and an ability to understand the needs of others. April demonstrated this interpersonal capacity in her relationship with Cathy, and the two children became inseparable. Shayne noted, "They're not really talking to each other a lot, but they are communicating a lot by being there for each other, by being together."

Similarly, Andrews (1995), in his ethnography of John Mcgough's life in Mendocino, California, described a sense of reciprocity on the part of John's friends in their relationships with him—something that had not existed in his segregated schooling. One of John's closest friends, a drummer in a local rock-and-roll band, explained:

> We have our basic core in common: We both love music and we both believe that everybody is part of the same family—and that music and communication and understanding and eventually peace, peaceful cooperation on earth, are all our goals. And so we have that in common, and that's really, for me, remarkable. I don't meet a whole lot of people that even consider such things, let alone a person like John who is totally into the movement toward life. (quoted in Andrews, 1995, p. 106)

John, in describing the drummer, noted, "We are just the same! Drink together, eat together, laugh contagious together. . . . We been learning about life together" (p. 106).

Defining Social Place: A Shared Location

A sense of reciprocity or shared value exists in relationships in which individuals, including those with the most severe disabilities, are recognized as thinking, feeling, caring human beings with personalities all their own. Though we may construe such traits to be intrinsic characteristics of the person that then set the conditions for citizenship, in actuality they cannot emerge, or indeed exist, apart from one's connection to the community. For instance, through his high school experience, John Mcgough was, in every negative sense of the metaphorical label, mentally retarded (Andrews, 1995). He scored poorly on intelligence tests; he had few realized community skills and rarely ventured far from his home except to go to his segregated school; and he had a distinct inability to communicate thoughts beyond the most rudimentary level. His existence was one of isolation and disconnection from everyone but his caring family.

His move to Mendocino shattered the image of John as a community burden. There he entered into relationships in which his individuality was both recognized and valued (Andrews, 1995). John was not forced to prove his competence to the Mendocino citizenry in the way schools had first demanded, then given up on. Rather, the townspeople assumed John's humanness, which led to community connections that further established his thoughtfulness, individuality, and community value. Andrews (1995) notes:

> By the end of John's first year in Mendocino he was holding down two part-time jobs; taking weekly voice, art, and guitar lessons; attending aerobics classes five mornings a week; occasionally reading stories to kids at the local preschool; helping his mother teach a class on self-esteem to a group of troubled adolescents; making daily visiting "rounds" in the community; and going out to dance or listen to music at least five nights a week. He had numerous friends and acquaintances, and he was daily becoming more verbal and more assertive. (p. 108)

Just one year earlier, John had been labeled "uneducable." John was, of course, still John, but in this new context he was anything but who he was perceived to be in North Hollywood.

John's hectic schedule, his work, his art, his enhanced communication—these were not the precursors to citizenship; rather, they were the consequences of his community connectedness. One's participation in the democratic experience exists not after the fact of cognitive development, communication skills development, demonstrations of competence, IQ scores above the magic number 70, or adaptive behavior acquisition, but serves as the terrain on which these various elements are realized. Vygotsky (1981) argued, "Social relations or relations among people genetically underlie all higher [human mental] functions and their relationships" (p. 163). He did not use the term "genetically" in its biological sense, but rather to suggest community as a point of origin in the development of higher-level intellect.

John's dramatic shift in persona is an example of *altered social place*—from a location of hopelessness to one filled with possibility (Bogdan & Taylor, 1989). Both his *social network* and *role* within the web of relationships from which community is formed were fundamentally transformed on his move to Mendocino. He left behind his community status of disconnected alien for a location of value and community membership. His experience demonstrates the power of context in the recognition of individual uniqueness and, in turn, how such recognition further recontextualizes one's social place.

Though John had to physically move far away from his formal education in order to find citizenship, numerous schools around the country, and indeed internationally, are restructuring in an effort to engage students with Down syndrome and other disabilities in the dialogue of democracy. These efforts to alter one's social place take shape in recontextualized curricula and a transformed conceptualization of communication.

Recontextualizing Curricula Toward Community. In her *Wild Thing* production (see above), Shayne Robbins clearly rejected the commonly held assumption that the school curriculum represents an objective knowledge base or set of skills initially disconnected from the child, who must then be manipulated along a rigid, linear, and individual path toward conformity. Instead, for Shayne, curriculum emerged from her students' daily lives in which they together gave meaning to classroom experiences. Understanding developed out of a constant process of negotiating and renegotiating relationships with peers, adults, and materials.

Shayne and her colleagues saw their role as one of creating a relatively safe community in which the children felt confident in formulating and reformulating their web of relationships. She explained:

> What's that one "saying"? "The dignity of risk." It's really true. That's what learning is. It's taking risks and seeing stuff in new ways. From the top of the slide [on the playground]. Or, like, in a book that you just open up. Those kinds of ways. Maybe you don't read the book exactly like the author wrote it, but you're making sense of it—like Isaac. Dancing to it, and then the next day, maybe your dance changes.

Shayne was not being metaphorical. Isaac literally danced to books, and his dance did change as books were discussed, acted out, reread, and discarded for new books. But Isaac's dance also changed how his peers and teachers saw the stories. Before encountering Isaac, few if any of the classroom community (including this researcher) realized you could actually dance to a book at all.

Isaac's literary waltzes established a new sense of communication that connected children, teachers, and materials in a manner that was previously nonexistent. In essence, and to a degree, communication conformed to Isaac. But this could only occur if Shayne was prepared to see Isaac as a human being and acknowledge in his idiosyncratic performance a desire and unique ability to connect to the community.

Shayne's intuitive sense of curriculum has been broadly described as *constructivist* in orientation (Poplin, 1988). In curricular constructivism, "the teacher is to develop experiences for students in the classroom that will spark their interest, connect to previous knowledge, and thus stimulate students to become actively involved in constructing new meanings for themselves" (Poplin, Wiest, & Thorson, 1996, p. 156). Fundamental to constructivist teaching is a respect for *each* student as both an active agent in the learning process and an essential member of the learning community.

Constructivist education directly reflects Vygotsky's sense of higher mental functions emerging through an individual's connection to the community. As Vygotsky (1981) explained, "Any higher mental function necessarily goes through an external stage in its development because it is initially a social function" (p. 162). It exists first on the cultural plane between people and is only internalized (and in the process, transformed) through a child's connection with others.

As such, education is considered a dual process of group and individual transformation through which children (1) establish together a unique community in thoughtfully planned activities, projects, experiences, and problems; and (2) support one another's membership in that community. The role of the teacher is to foster and guide the children's efforts, and to create a reflective dimension to schooling that allows children to critically consider and interpret the meaning of their contribution to the transformation of community. For instance, in the *Wild Thing* production, Shayne facilitated a student-inspired conversation on why girls might just as easily be Max as boys. "Who here hasn't gotten in trouble?" she asked, "Who here hasn't felt sad when you're away from your mom?" Certain of the children's fundamental orientations toward gender differences were dramatically challenged in both the act of creating the play through roles shared by the sexes and in talking openly about the idea that roles might be shared at all.

A constructivist curriculum not only realizes a Vygotskian sense of community acting as the foundation of individual development but also makes school a place where it is possible to recognize Gardner's broadened framework of intellect. In his call for the restructuring of schools for *all* children, Gardner proposed a conceptualization of curriculum based on the dynamic, student-directed model of hands-on museums. This, he suggested, would be fostered by teachers taking on the role of mentor in a disciplined and rigorous apprenticeship process. He notes:

> As early as the first grade, Japanese students are posed arithmetical problems of some complexity and allowed up to a week to solve the problems. They are encouraged to work together, to criticize one another's approaches, and to try out different roles vis-à-vis the problem. Teachers deliberately avoid serving as a source of answers, although they may coach, direct, or probe in various ways. (Gardner, 1991, p. 221)

In this way, students not only come to understand mathematics (or other content areas) as an active process—a conversation (Greeno, 1988) between one's self and the environment—but they also discover the benefits of working together as a community.

Constructivist curricula may take shape in an emergent form, as happened in Shayne Robbins's classroom, but they also fit somewhat more traditional instructional arrangements. Harris (1994), in her ethnography of Christine Durovich, describes one such merger of constructivism with a more traditional curriculum. Christine, a young woman with Down syndrome, had gone through segregated schooling until the age of 14, when her mother demanded an end to her daughter's isolation from the community.

When she enrolled in a regular public high school as a freshman, Christine's Individual Education Plan was passed on from her segregated school; it suggested that she had extremely poor motor control, low-level cognitive skills, low-level communication skills, a lack of adaptive skills, and aggressive "acting-out" behaviors. In the general curriculum of the regular high school, however, these images of defect were dramatically transformed (Harris, 1994).

In her freshman year, Christine's fine and gross motor skills improved in keyboarding classes, home economics, and regular physical education. In science classes, she not only learned properties of the physical world but also addressed personal safety and health concerns. Reading, writing, and mathematics skills developed in school and in vocationally based community activities. When she was out in the community, Christine's social network broadened to include merchants for whom she worked, store clerks from whom she made purchases, and bus drivers who got her around town. The community-based program was not created for Christine; rather, it was an option for all the school's students who could benefit from vocational opportunities outside school.

Christine's communication skills also improved dramatically. Her teachers suggested that Christine's enhanced speech was a product of the necessity of engaging in conversations and also reflected, interestingly, her participation on the cheerleading squad. Christine had enrolled too late for cheerleading try-outs, but she accepted a position as manager of the squad. In this capacity, she not only was responsible for organizing practices but also joined in the drills, chants, and songs. In a sense, this form of repetitive expression acted as a powerful form of speech therapy designed in dialogue between Christine and her new network of friends (Harris, 1994). In conjunction with improved communication and an expanded social network, school personnel noted a dramatic decrease in Christine's aggressive behaviors.

In her sophomore year, Christine enrolled in a journalism class whose members were responsible for publishing the school's newspaper. Christine joined the efforts to meet deadlines, space requirements, editorial standards, and quality reporting of school and community news. Eventually, she was given a weekly column, "Christine's Corner," in which she addressed important educational issues. One column struck out at a school district's refusal to allow a student with cerebral palsy to enroll in a nonsegregated school. Christine wrote:

> Knock it off! Knock it off! Becky is a girl who has cerebral palsy. . . . She's not allowed in school because of her handicaps. I think her school should just knock it off and let her in.
>
> She needs an education. Just because she is handicapped doesn't mean she can't learn. She's just got to do what she can do, which can be just about anything.
>
> Becky is smart enough to fight back, just like I would if I wasn't allowed in school. I have Down syndrome and I can still do anything I want to do. If I wasn't allowed in school, I wouldn't have learned to do all the things I do now. I have Down syndrome, but I am not handicapped. (Durovich, 1990, quoted in Harris, 1994, p. 296)

Christine's social place continued to be transformed through her involvement in a high school curriculum that reflected her interests and needs as well as being based on community. In turn, Christine also transformed the culture of the school and community. For instance, she set up a weekly teaching seminar for third graders in which she addressed health and safety concerns. In doing so, she had to further refine her articulation and behavior. Her peers at school also felt Christine's influence. One high-status student, Bubba, an excellent athlete, got to know Christine through their work on the school paper, and he joined her struggle to allow Becky, the young woman with cerebral palsy, to enter school. Bubba traveled to Toronto, Canada, to speak to a gathering of school personnel on the issue of Becky's right to an education in a regular setting. A teacher commented, "I used to see [Bubba] as a jock who never looked past Friday's game. Now I notice a young man with empathy and a sense of responsibility for others" (quoted in Harris, 1994, p. 296).

Christine's high school experience, dramatically different from what the segregated school offered, was not so different from that of nondisabled students. Through thoughtful planning constructed on the foundation of community, Christine entered the dialogic of democracy with a vengeance. In her school and community participation, she gained status as a valuable human being, a social place her mother had realized was Christine's right all along.

Transforming Communication. A curriculum built on community that leads to individual development and group transformation realigns traditional interpretations of communication. Special education has long held onto a model that suggests communication is an act that involves two or more parties in which information is encoded, sent, received, and decoded (Heward, 1996). Each of these elements of communication is considered a distinct aspect of an individual's intrinsic communicative ability. If a misunderstanding emerges within the act of communication, we tend to fault the party with the least amount of cultural privilege and proceed to clinically identify which element of that individual's communication is responsible for the misunderstanding.

Constructivism rejects this simplistic model. It recognizes that communication is a shared process of interpretation in which dialogue of any type builds on itself, twists, turns, and reformulates the relationship with each new utterance, each wave of the hand, twitch of the eyebrow, or twist of the mouth (Duchan, 1993). If a misunderstanding emerges, its cause is not located in any individual but in the communicative web that connects all of us to one another. As such, the label "communication-disordered" attached to any individual makes no sense. It is not the individual who owns the problem; rather, the dilemma exists in the interconnected relationships that both form and hinder community.

When Lee Larson entered Colleen Madison's second-grade classroom, he was unable to speak. Speech was the privileged modality for community connectedness that precluded Lee's entry into certain relationships and resulted in a context of trepidation. Colleen noted, "We were always walking on pins and needles waiting for the other shoe to drop. We never knew when he was going to erupt."

Rather than suggesting that Lee was at fault for instilling fear into the class, Colleen explained, "We knew communication was the big piece missing. He was frustrated. We quickly saw that he gestured to try to tell us things. We understood him best through motion and movement." Based on his manner of performance, Colleen invited a parent of one of her students to come each week to teach all her students signed English. The parent read books and signed along to the text; she engaged the class in conversation and demonstrated signs as the discussion progressed.

Lee's teachers began to sign key words in lessons and, as he became comfortable with signs, in conversation. Lee quickly began to gesture with close approximation to the signed English script. Colleen said, "We thought, 'Wow! We can understand Lee better when he's signing and doing these motions.' It sort of clicked with him." As Lee's proficiency with signed English increased, his aggressive tantrums decreased.

In providing Lee with a set of shared symbols to convey ideas, Colleen had recontextualized the communicative context of the classroom in a constructivist manner. She took Lee's idiosyncratic performance mannerisms and experiences seriously, recognizing in Lee a thinking, affective, valuable individual whose ability to connect with his community could occur only after he was afforded membership. (The centrality of communication to citizenship will be expanded on in the following chapter, which looks closely at literacy acquisition in students with Down syndrome.)

CONCLUDING THOUGHTS ON SCHOOL CITIZENSHIP AND THE RECONCEPTUALIZATION OF DOWN SYNDROME

Educating all children together reconfigures the representation of Down syndrome from burden toward citizenship. Isaac Johnson, April Carpenter, Lee Larson, John Mcgough, Christine Durovich, and others engaged in the struggle as dialogic participants in the web of relationships from which community is constructed. Through citizenship, they came to be recognized as thinking, creative individuals who added unique and valuable dimensions to the group. To reiterate, such recognition does not constitute the condition on which judgments of membership are based. Rather, citizenship by right is the core from which human value emerges. At the same time, citizenship is based on an assumption of human value. It is a reciprocal relationship and can only be understood as such.

One can visualize the reconceptualization of Down syndrome and disability by returning to the metaphor of the gap first described in Chapter 3. Community banishment of students with Down syndrome stems from their lack of behavioral and communicative conformity to school standards that form the parameters of intellectual normality. In essence, a gap exists between the performance of students with Down syndrome and the performance expectations that define a useful individual. Students with Down syndrome are placed in school structures that supposedly remediate their defects in order that they can eventually join the wider community. But this, of course, leads to perpetual school separation and, ultimately, the need for community placements that mirror the rigidity of segregated special education.

School citizenship rejects the idea of a gap between normality and Down syndrome. In the movement toward classroom membership, "diversity is viewed as normal, people are considered of equal worth, relationships are of mutual benefit, and belonging is a central societal theme" (Van der Klift & Kunc, 1994, p. 396). Community is not a location within circled wagons configured to keep out those charged with having the differences that matter. It is instead a web of dynamic, constantly shifting relationships that encompass the individual with Down syndrome and all other human beings. To eliminate a single person through any form of banishment, no matter how benevolent the logic, reduces the web and makes the community a less democratic and less rich place.

As mentioned earlier, people with Down syndrome are joined in their struggle for citizenship by other oppressed groups. In Chapter 2, I recounted how home economics emerged in conjunction with compulsory education laws as a public school location engineered to maintain young women in a devalued social place. Though covert devaluation of girls in school continues, educational and community opportunities have greatly expanded (including within the study of home economics itself). This shift toward the realization of citizenship was not simply handed to women. It has been a hard-fought struggle for democracy spearheaded by the women's movement. In its effort to achieve social justice, the movement has not simply re-created women to look more like men; instead it has challenged the very foundation of community that sets up particular gendered relationships as more valued than others. In so doing, it has transformed society, though the struggle continues as full community membership for traditionally devalued groups remains elusive.

5

Citizenship in the Literate Community: Down Syndrome, Communication, and the Written Word

Ruth, a young woman with Down syndrome living in Israel, spent most of her school years in a location of hopelessness similar to John Mcgough's (see Chapter 4) prior to his move to Mendocino (Andrews, 1995). People around Ruth perceived her to be "completely illiterate and diagnosed [her] as severely mentally retarded. No functional comprehension was considered possible for her" (Feuerstein, Rand, & Rynders, 1988, p. 37). Ruth's education eventually came under the guidance of Reuven Feuerstein, an educator and psychologist who firmly rejected the notion that Ruth or, for that matter, any human being was intrinsically intellectually defective (Feuerstein, Rand, & Hoffman, 1979; Tzuriel, 1992). Feuerstein acknowledged that certain people's performance and behavior may lead others to infer that the individual is cognitively deficient, but this inference in no way represents the person's capacity to conceptualize and know the world in complex and meaningful ways.

Instructors who worked alongside Feuerstein altered Ruth's hopeless social place. They immersed her in a context of thoughtful expectations that took seriously her performance differences and supported her connection to the wider social world. Over the course of 3 years of schooling, Ruth's life dramatically changed: "She learned to read, write, and travel by herself. . . . Ruth has become a proficient individual, able to converse fluently on topics such as literature and art, citing the many books she has read" (Feuerstein et al., 1988, pp. 37–38).

The transformation in the perception of Ruth from an illiterate burden to a literate human being was in no way miraculous; rather, it represented a thoughtful reorientation of the context surrounding her. She was first connected to the community; on that foundation, new opportunities allowed Ruth to engage in and express literacies originally deemed inaccessible to anyone as mentally retarded as she was assumed to be. In turn, Ruth's community connections were further enhanced by her interpretations of books she had read and the insights and discussions they generated.

CITIZENSHIP AND LITERACY

The many years Ruth spent labeled "illiterate" stemmed from a lack of opportunity to engage in meaningful reading experiences within a framework of thoughtful expectations. Many students with Down syndrome, existing apart from the literate community as educational aliens or squatters, experience similar forms of socially imposed illiteracy (Buckley, 1985, 1995; Oelwein, 1995).

Traditions of Separation: Imposing Illiteracy

Two cultural assumptions merge as the justification for denying students with Down syndrome the right to read. The first has to do with how we conceptualize the act of reading itself. The prevailing school representation of language literacy suggests it is one isolated content area of a segmented curriculum constructed on a set of linear and hierarchial subskills (Adams, 1990; O'Donnell & Wood, 1992). The assumption suggests that these subskills have been scientifically deduced, logically arranged, and must be taught directly to students or discovered by them in correct order through teacher-crafted, carefully contrived activities. Those students who demonstrate at an age-normed pace what is assumed to be a cognitively based conformity to the reading subskills are defined as citizens of the literate community. Conformity is generally measured through paper-and-pencil assessments, workbook assignments, spoken responses to teacher questions, or reading out loud.

The second assumption, which merges with the first to act as a rationale for segregating students with Down syndrome from the literate community, is based on the commutative law of Down syndrome (see Chapter 3). This suggests that children with trisomy-21 are inherently cognitively impaired. Thus, their lack of conformity to the sequence of literacy subskills is assumed to be of intellectual origins, and they are often retained at rudimentary levels of the subskill hierarchy—if they are allowed on the reading ladder at all.

Joanna Sylvester, a 9-year-old with Down syndrome, experienced a disconnection from literacy opportunities in her primary years at school. She was introduced in Chapter 3 in a squatter's position on the curricula periphery of her regular second-grade class. Joanna's speech and movement control were very different from those of her classmates, who participated in a three-tiered reading instruction format. Each tier was represented by a single reading group composed of children thought to be reading and writing at a particular level. The top tier was considered the most advanced, with each successively lower tier containing students less able to conform to the scope and sequence of the advanced group's reading level.

Joanna was nonspeaking. Her movements were slow and awkward. When she walked, she alternated attention between moving her limbs and avoiding obstacles. She formed a fist to grasp a pencil and had difficulty regulating the pressure necessary to write. Her papers often ended up ripped and uninterpretable.

Joanna's movement and speech did not conform to traditional expectations for how a competent student should look or sound. Her performance mannerisms led to teacher assumptions that she lacked the intellectual abilities necessary to participate in any of the three reading groups, which were based on mastering the basal series' scope and sequence. Instead, Joanna and her four peers with disabilities were combined into a "print awareness" group. During reading and language arts periods, Joanna's group went from the classroom to the hall, where a teaching assistant, Mrs. Capo, read to them from oversized books (called "Big Books").

At times Mrs. Capo asked individual students to stand beside her and recite words from the text she was reading. Joanna was invited to stand beside Mrs. Capo but was not expected to enunciate words. Following the reading, the children laid on the floor and colored in dittos of pictures related to the story. Joanna had extreme difficulty using crayons in a normative manner; she was regarded as the least literate child in this group of children all considered to lack literacy abilities.

On several occasions, however, Joanna stood beside Mrs. Capo with eyes focused on the book's text, softly articulating the final word of each sentence prior to or in unison with Mrs. Capo. This suggested three very real and exciting possibilities: (1) Joanna was able to read words; (2) her articulation was cued by print (see Buckley, 1995); and (3) she needed the time Mrs. Capo spent reading the first part of the sentence to physically prepare herself to enunciate the final word. Mrs. Capo disagreed with my interpretation: "Joanna wasn't reading then," she smiled, "she makes those sounds like a kid playing school." Considering Joanna as literate was kindly dismissed; her idiosyncratic behaviors and appearance precluded any possibility of her membership in the reading community.

Breaking with Tradition: Reconceptualizing the Literate Community

In contrast to Joanna Sylvester's separation from the literate community, certain teachers, many of whom were described in Chapter 4, reject the two premises that merge to create school-imposed illiteracy. They do not see reading as an end-product of a linear, transmitted set of subskills that, when mastered, set the conditions for acceptance into the literate community. Nor do they accept the social inference of intellectual ineptitude as an intrinsic and delimiting characteristic of students with Down syndrome. Instead, all children are considered active participants in the construction of literate meanings within specific contexts. This assumption of literate value then serves as the core from which literate capacities are realized.

Human Reciprocity and the Assumption of Literate Value. Shayne Robbins at the Shoshone School noted, "I see all my kids as incredible readers. Every one of them." Though her students were preschoolers and most did not demonstrate print-decoding skills commonly associated with school definitions of *reading*, Shayne was firmly convinced that each child was an active participant in the construction of symbolic meaning in the contexts of their everyday lives. The children's processes of building understanding took shape in the stories they told through the many texts of childhood, including spoken language, play, tears, tantrums, paintings, projects, and hugs.

Stories are never constructed in isolation. They *connect* one person with another; they are fundamentally communication, and the children's texts must be acknowledged, heard, and understood as such. Reading, then, in the framework of human reciprocity, is an act of communication, interpretation, and transformation; it is story telling *and* it is story hearing. This latter act, in and of itself, exerts influence on the stories told. It communicates back to the story teller, "You are worth listening to." That simple statement sets the conditions for negotiating and renegotiating relationships of mutual respect in a direction of shared understanding. It establishes a reciprocal belief in the ability to think, express, and be understood on the part of all classroom participants.

In her insightful framework for developing literacy skills in children with Down syndrome, Oelwein (1995) noted that interaction is the basis of literacy: "A child cannot learn . . . if her efforts to communicate are not 'read' and responded to, and if she does not 'read' and respond to the communication of others" (p. 13). Shayne Robbins explained, "My sense is not that I'm teaching anyone to read, but I'm showing them that they do know how to read—to have them feel comfortable that they do read. What they do, and this is so central, they are making sense of it all."

In her assumption that all children had literate value, Shayne reconfigured the foundation of reading. She did not interpret written language abilities as emerging from a core of isolated subskills that, once demonstrated at age-appropriate levels, then set the condition for membership in the literate community. Rather, she recognized the need to assume membership in the collective first, and that then, *and only then*, could an individual child's symbolic and interpretive capacities be realized.

Had Shayne maintained a need for her student Isaac Johnson to demonstrate the varied subskills delineated by developmental checklists as precursors to reading, Isaac would not have been included as a citizen of the literate community, nor would he have played a central role in the creation of the class's *Wild Thing* production (see Chapter 4). In fact, the *Wild Thing* production might never have occurred at all. Isaac's manner of behavior, his idiosyncratic modes of communication, his trisonomy-21 phenotype—all this could (and, for many, often does) merge to effectively remove him from classroom opportunities to engage with the stories of childhood, whether told by classmates, by Isaac himself, or discovered in the richness of children's literature.

Shayne's intuitive recognition of the literate dimension of her students was not necessarily shared by her colleagues and associates. Rather, it appeared to emerge from a reflectiveness on her part and became established over time and in critical dialogue with her students and co-workers. During circle time one morning, Shayne held up flashcards showing the children's names; each child's name was printed on a separate flashcard. On recognizing his or her name, the child stood, retrieved the card, and placed it in an attendance pile. As a classmate stood to get her card, Isaac lifted himself up and stumbled toward Shayne. Wendy, an associate, sharply whispered, "Isaac, you sit back down. It's April's turn." Isaac froze. Shayne glanced over, read the situation, and quickly said, "Isaac, you saw your name was next in the pile. Come on up." Isaac looked back at Wendy. She told him, "Oh, go on then." But he appeared stuck and simply sat down in the middle of the circle.

The result was an appearance of incompetence, with Isaac seated alone in the middle of the circle while his classmates looked on in confusion. Shayne understood his initial actions to be a self-created compensation for awkward and slow movements. But his efforts were cut short. Shayne, however, recognized that an adult's ability to interpret Isaac as a constructive, purposeful learner required the same sort of guidance she provided her young students. She could not simply tell people, "Look, the kid can think." Rather, she had to show them. She recounted a similar experience with a different classroom associate, Jennifer Perry, who initially believed Isaac's classmate, Lisa Kelly, who also had Down syndrome, could not read.

Lisa's parents recognized her ability to read books at home and wanted the classroom to address specific reading skills that would help her to appear competent when she entered regular public school. Jennifer, however, resisted the parents' wishes that their daughter's Individual Education Plan (IEP) include reading objectives. Shayne noted with slight sarcasm:

Jennifer didn't have an indication that Lisa knew all her colors, and you know all those prerequisites that are so important to reading! (Shayne laughed.) But Bill [Lisa's father] and Jennifer had this really involved discussion about it, and Jennifer had really said that she didn't want to set Lisa up to fail. That she didn't want to put in goals that she wasn't going to accomplish.

Lisa's father, Bill, compromised and agreed that the IEP goals should reflect lower-level skills than he had originally requested, but Jennifer was quickly confronted in the classroom by Lisa's ability to read books out loud. This skill was difficult to dispute, and it forced Jennifer to reinterpret her image of Lisa. In one field observation occurring several months into the school year, I watched Dan, a nondisabled classmate of Lisa's, work independently at a "rhyming center." He glued words written on small squares of paper to a worksheet divided in half. On one side went the words that rhymed with *cat* and on the other side went the words that rhymed with *fish*. Lisa approached the center, reached into the basket that contained the word squares, and inadvertently crumpled a fistful. This upset Dan, but Jennifer quickly moved in. She recognized Lisa's difficulty with fine motor tasks and helped her smooth the scraps. She placed the word *rat* in front of Lisa and said, "Does this rhyme with *fish* or *cat*?" Lisa pointed to *cat* on the worksheet, then said, "Cat." Together, Lisa and Jennifer glued the word to the sheet. Dan left his work and joined the two. Jennifer, after getting to know Lisa, no longer interpreted her as incompetent but rather assumed she had a place in the literate community and provided her with support that allowed her to demonstrate her print abilities.

Lisa's ability to speak to convey her written language skills in turn influenced the classroom personnel's interpretation of the students who were nonspeaking. Shayne explained:

If you watch Lisa in our room, it makes it a lot less hard to understand how Isaac can spell words to communicate because Lisa, who can speak better, can read lots of things out loud, and it's a really important cue for her.

Lisa's literate capacities, impossible to deny due to her speech, suggested that print was an accessible language modality for all young children's communication and was perhaps an important symbolic cue for spoken language in students whose speech was limited or nonexistent (see Buckley, 1995, and below for an affirmation of this).

Recognizing a literate dimension in all children serves as the terrain on which written language capacities are realized. This was dramatically reflected in one segregated classroom for students defined as having autism (Koppenhaver, Pierce, & Yoder, 1995). Special education professionals had described six of the seven children in the class as having moderate to severe cognitive impairments and no functional written language skills. The children's classroom literacy opportunities had been limited to sporadic copying tasks and some sight-word instructional drills. One consequence of segregation is often a lack of the literature and print opportunities common to the school lives of nondisabled children.

During a 6-week summer session at the school, a graduate student from a nearby university took over the class in the role of lead teacher. Over the course of her brief stay, she opened up classroomwide literacy opportunities that enabled every child in the room to demonstrate capacities in the use and comprehension of print. Several students engaged language in a manner that directly contradicted their labels of "severe mental retardation."

Nathan, for instance, an 8-year-old child considered to have severe cognitive impairments who was nonspeaking and aggressive, was given, along with all his other classmates, a journal in which to write (Koppenhaver et al., 1995). Initially, he copied text from the classroom walls. His teacher then showed him pictures related to his everyday life and asked that he write about them. Independent of support, he proceeded to generate written labels describing the pictures. Another student, a 7-year-old who was deemed nonverbal and defined as unable to comprehend text, demonstrated reading and comprehension skills *through spoken language* at a fourth-grade level. This occurred only after the teacher had engaged the class with books of interest to them and had incorporated the use of favorite television shows in her literacy planning (Koppenhaver et al., 1995).

No piece of school information provided to the graduate-student-turned-teacher suggested these children could or would demonstrate written language abilities. Their permanent files were as hopeless as were John Mcgough's and Christine Durovich's (introduced in Chapter 4) before they escaped their segregated education. Recall that within 1 year of leaving behind his formal school label of "uneducable," John was reading weekly to preschoolers (Andrews, 1995; see Chapter 4). Two years after entering her regular high school, Christine was writing a weekly column in the school paper (Harris, 1994; see Chapter 4). They found *connection.* Similarly, the six students in the segregated autism class found connection to the literate community at the invitation of the graduate student. She, like Shayne Robbins, intuitively recognized the children's value and right to belong. One shudders, though, when considering that her stay was only 6 weeks long.

The Literate Relationship: Written Language as a Tool. Realizing the literate dimension of human reciprocity reshapes the appearance of written language competence. The metaphor of the ladder leading to the act of reading no longer makes sense. Rather, literacy takes on the shape of the community. It becomes a web of shifting relationships as expansive as the appearance of the citizenry itself. No one, no matter how idiosyncratic his or her connection, is left out.

In this framework, the role of the teacher is that of guide. She or he leads the students who make up the literate web through thoughtful experiences that re-form their relationships in a direction of enhanced connection. As guides, teachers recognize that connecting over shared meaning is fostered when children conform at some level to patterns of communication that others can decipher with minimal struggle. Reading, as a form of "complex communication" (Oelwein, 1995, p. 13), requires shared patterns of symbol use. Conformity, however, is a consequence of citizenship; it is not a precursor, and it evolves positively only when communication is understood to be a reciprocal process of interaction. Listening constitutes as active an effort as does expression; indeed, listening *is* expression.

Paradoxically, communicative conformity also is transformative: The expressive, interpretive path is not rigid, narrow, or static but expands to merge with the child's uniquenesses to create a shared, albeit shifting, connection with the wider community. For instance, Isaac's dancing to books became a classroomwide mode for interpreting children's literature (see Chapter 4). His dance conveyed meaning to those around him, who picked up on the dance and began to communicate in a similar fashion.

In most classrooms, speech is established as the primary and privileged method for building relationships, and this includes within the literate community. O'Donnell and Wood (1992), for instance, describe their developmental reading process as applicable only to preschool students with "well developed oral language" and "extensive listening/speaking vocabularies" (p. 15). As a result, children with Down syndrome, whose speech is often difficult to interpret if it exists at all, commonly find themselves pushed to the classroom periphery even after spending years in remedial speech therapy (see Chapters 3 and 4).

Rather than maintaining students with Down syndrome in stagnant relationships of elusive meaning and misunderstanding, certain teachers have turned to symbols other than speech, including written language, as an alternative communication mode for connecting children with the wider community (Abrahamsen, Romski, & Sevak, 1989; Crossley, 1994; Meyers, 1986; Pecyna, 1988). Use of communication alternatives is based on a school community that assumes the students' literate value and rejects the representation of reading as an end-product of an isolated content area. The written word becomes a tool in the struggle of meaning itself. It is recognized as communication and is used as such.

Powerful results for children, disabled or not, have been reported when teachers engage literacy as a mode of interaction and meaning construction rather than as an isolated set of skills that must be mastered in order for the student to advance to the next basal-established reading level (Ashton-Warner, 1963; Cunningham & Allington, 1994; F. Smith, 1988a, 1988b; Solsken, 1993). Ashton-Warner (1963), for instance, described her work with minority-culture kindergartners in New Zealand. Her Maori students' reading skills fell far behind the skills of students from the dominant Western culture. The school system's primary explanation for this discrepancy laid blame on the Maori population's presumed genetic inferiority. Ashton-Warner, however, recognized that the basal system used for literacy instruction held little relevance to the Maori children's lives. She threw out the workbooks and stale texts, and initiated a literacy program in which students learned to read through telling and writing stories from their own experiences. The stories were then translated into conventional writing. By the end of their kindergarten year, Ashton-Warner's students demonstrated reading and writing skills at extremely advanced levels. She explained that the single most important dimension to becoming a reader and writer was to discover print as a mode of communication. Literacy, according to Ashton-Warner (1963), develops only when it is used to communicate important, relevant thoughts.

More recently, Gardner has concurred with Ashton-Warner's perception of written language as communication. He points out that educators have traditionally relied so heavily on phonics that children are left with little understanding of *why* they should read to begin with or to what ends reading might lead. He suggests that reading must emerge from a sense of its communicative potential in literate classrooms where "children read not because they are told—let alone ordered!—to read, but because they see adults around them reading, enjoying their reading, and using that reading productively for their own purposes" as a tool of connection (1991, p. 212) "Children who are successful at becoming literate," note Cunningham and Allington (1994), "view reading and writing as authentic activities from which they get information and pleasure and by which they communicate with others"(p. 21).

In Chapter 4, I described Lee Larson entering Colleen Madison's second-grade classroom with extremely limited systematic communication abilities. Colleen quickly recognized Lee's ability to convey meaning through movement, and I described her insertion of signed English into the normal course of classroom teaching and conversation. Signing is, of course, far less complex motorically than is speech production, and it has been recognized as a viable communicative alternative for students with Down syndrome who consistently demonstrate movement dilemmas

(Gibbs, Springer, Cooley, & Gray, 1993; Kumin, 1994). Kumin (1994) noted that "it is often easier [for children with Down syndrome] to recognize and make gestures with their hands than it is for them to make speech sounds" (p. 57). Lee began to gesture using sign approximations, and his ability to convey requests improved.

Colleen, though, was not yet satisfied. She recognized the benefits of signing for Lee, but she felt the fine motor control required to manipulate his hands drew energy away from his ability to formulate and meaning-fully convey thoughts beyond simple requests stuck in the here-and-now. She said, "It's like when you're learning to drive stick-shift. It's all you can do to steer, shift, break, turn, let alone figure out where you're going."

Drake (1993) used a similar metaphor in his description of Case, Kurland, and Goldberg's (1982) model of intellectual development. Case and colleagues (1982) suggested that human beings have, at any given point in their development, a finite cognitive *space* for total central processing. This area is divided between the hypothetical space available to store in-formation and the hypothetical operating space used for executing intel-lectual processes. According to Case and colleagues (1982), as the operat-ing space develops in efficiency, it requires less of the processing area, which allows the space allotted for the storage of information to expand. Drake (1993) explained:

> One way to think about this is to think back to the time when first learning to drive a car. This activity generally demands the total concentration of novice drivers. Even as ease increases on familiar roads, attentional demands sharply increase when a new driver hits an expressway for the first time. Anyone who has worked with a new driver has found that it is useless to give verbal directions all at once. . . . One must give new drivers directions one step at a time, as the demands of driving get in the way of holding all that information and retrieving it in a timely manner. (p. 4)

Colleen likened Lee's signing to demands placed on a new driver. She described Lee as "bogged down" by sign language: "I mean, have you ever seen the sign for butterfly? I even have to stop and figure out where my fingers are going! Imagine what it's like for Lee." Shayne Robbins, a part-time American Sign Language interpreter, also conveyed frustration with sign language for her students with Down syndrome. For instance, April Carpenter's primary mode of communication was signed English, but the physical requirements posed a potential and impending barrier. Shayne explained:

> Like, April is really into signs, but until her fine motor skills im-prove from where they're at right now, she's going to reach a limit

in terms of how well she communicates because her signs look very similar to each other. That is true of a lot of our kids, but the difference is they don't need to sign to be understood. So there's going to need to be something else for her pretty soon because otherwise she's going to be frustrated. She's going to be communicating and we're not going to be understanding.

Both Shayne and Colleen, realizing their students' literate value, turned to written language as an alternative form of expression. Colleen noted that even though the instructional team recognized Lee as literate in the context of curricular assignments, they still hesitated at the idea of using print to foster connections among Lee, his peers, and the wider community. The commutative law of Down syndrome posed a potential attitudinal barrier. Colleen said:

There's baggage involved. I had to sit down with myself and say, "Now look, Lee needs to express himself. He's frustrated. You've been surprised before." He needed a way to talk and talking wasn't going to cut it, and here was a potential way if I could just say, "Go for it!"

Colleen first introduced Lee to what she called a "communication board." Rather than configuring complex signs, Lee could simply point to an option. On the communication board was printed an array of words and phrases that might fit a variety of situations including: *yes, no, more, all done, bathroom, I need a break,* and *I don't know.* Colleen did not make Lee demonstrate phonic skills associated with decoding the words and phrases prior to their use but rather introduced them in a communicative framework using real choice opportunities. For instance, in a mathematics lesson, Lee was asked to point to a number line to express his answer. When it appeared he had gestured incorrectly, Colleen or a classroom associate held up the communication board and asked, "Is that your answer, Lee? Did you mean 12?" Within a week, Lee consistently used the phrases presented to him in meaningful, expressive ways. The classroom staff then created a series of communication boards to fit different situations and times of the day.

Colleen's next concern, however, focused on the inherent limitations imposed on Lee's communication when what he said hinged on a teacher-created set of phrases. Lee's quickly gained adeptness with print suggested that, intellectually, he might just as easily be able to produce phrases himself. However, his typing was hindered by both an erratic ability to initiate a pointing gesture and, once initiated, the explosive impulsivity of his movement patterns. Lee's finger, after he struggled to get it to move at all, would slam down on a keyboard with a bang, and it would remain there, fixed to a key, or to several keys, with multiple letters rapidly appearing across the screen.

Rather than seeing Lee's movements as representing incompetence, Colleen focused on the typing context. She recognized that the demands of typing did not match Lee's fine and gross motor abilities. So she altered the demands. First, she placed a keyguard over the keyboard to assist Lee in targeting individual letters. She then began a training process to develop his pointing abilities. In situations in which Lee was asked to type to convey information, Colleen supported his arm with her hand, helping him to pull his finger away from the keyboard after a selection was made. Her physical support assisted him in initiating gestures by apparently helping him isolate the muscles required to reach forward. It also slowed his movements and focused his attention on the target. Colleen explained, "It occurred to me he really needed the processing time, delay time, lag time. Overcome that impulsivity. And then stuff took off from there."

A similar form of training was described by Feuerstein and colleagues (1988). They noted in their work with people with Down syndrome that "many children who manifest impulsivity fail in tasks even though they know what they need to do to respond correctly" (p. 75). They suggest that certain students must be taught impulse control:

> At certain stages in the development of control over impulsivity, the mediator may need to use physical means to keep the child from impulsive responding—perhaps holding the child's hands (or asking the child to sit on his own hands)—so that he won't point to an answer before looking carefully at the situation and thinking about it. (p. 75)

The authors also noted movement initiation dilemmas on the part of children: "An individual may have perceived the problem adequately; he may even have a proper answer, but he is unable to answer either because of inhibition due to feelings of incompetence or because of difficulties in initiating a specific behavior" (p. 75). One child "required an outside 'trigger' in the form of a movement imposed on him" in order that he initiate a pointing gesture (p. 33). They explained that for this particular boy, "Verbal instructions, even with accompanying gestures, were not sufficient. Furthermore, a behavior, once triggered, required continued stimulation in order for it to be maintained" (p. 33).

Other researchers have also documented that a teacher's physical support appears to assist the development of controlled gestures on the part of students with Down syndrome (Anwar & Hermelin, 1979; Pecyna, 1988). Pecyna (1988) described a preschool student with Down syndrome who pointed to Rebus symbols to convey requests. Initially, the child required hand-over-hand support to reach out and target the correct symbol. Over time, the physical support was slowly reduced as the student's pointing skills increased. Eventually, the student required only an adult's presence to initiate movement. Anwar and Hermelin (1979) found that people with Down syndrome had extreme difficulty adapting the angle of their gestures when targets were laid out in close approximation, as are letters on a keyboard. Once a gesture was made in a particular direction, altering the angle for the next gesture proved problematic. Physical support by a second person helped the subjects redirect their movement.

Lee Larson's movement training program, described recently as an element of *facilitated communication training* (Crossley, 1994), led him to, as Colleen put it, "Take off." His gestures became increasingly controlled, and he was able to unhinge his communication from the phrases laid out by teachers. For instance, Lee and a classmate, Laura, got into an altercation on the classroom's couch. Laura shouted out, "Lee hit me." An assistant teacher, Leah George, asked, "Do you know why he hit you?" Laura responded, "I didn't do nothing." However, Lee was able to type on a keyboard, "I HIT LAR MAKE ME MOVE." Colleen, who had entered the situation, asked Laura, "Did you make Lee move?" Laura said, "I didn't make him. I *asked* him." Lee typed, "LARA MEAN", but the two quickly joined each other, giggling, in a beanbag chair.

The development of controlled gestures for communication purposes has been a source of some recent controversy in the disability professions (see, for example, a series of opinions published in 1994 in the American Association on Mental Retardation's journal *Mental Retardation*, 32[2]). The question emerges: In his movement training, when Lee types on a keyboard, is Colleen actually directing his hand? For Lee, the question was a moot point; his typing was so physically powerful that those observing recognized Colleen's minimal support could not force Lee's hand in any direction, let alone to a particular letter she had chosen. Lee also was able to convey information that was unknown to the person supporting the typing, which rendered impossible any charge of manipulation. For instance, he typed to Colleen one morning, "MOM MAD (.) BROKE LEVIN HE HIT ME (.)" Colleen spoke with Lee's mother and found out that Lee and his brother, Kevin, had been rough-housing at home. Their play turned aggressive and a knick-knack had been broken, resulting in both boys being sent to their rooms.

Nevertheless, the question of who is actually typing has led professionals to deny many students a training program they need in order to achieve their communicative potential. Ostensibly, the decision to deny children with motor problems access to literacy-based communication is tied to a series of studies that suggest students' gestures are being manipulated (Eberlin, McConnachie, Ibel, & Volpe, 1993; Hudson, Melita, & Arnold, 1993; Moore, Donovan, & Hudson, 1993; Simon, Toll, & Whitehair, 1994; Simpson & Myles, 1995; Szempruch & Jacobson, 1993; Wheeler, Jacobson, Paglieri, & Schwartz, 1993). However, basing decisions on these studies requires ignoring a vast amount of research that documents the communicative gestures as originating with the student (D. Biklen & Cardinal, 1997; Botash et al., 1994; Cardinal, Hanson, & Wakeham, 1996; IDRP, 1989; Janzen-Wilde, Duchan, & Higgenbotham, 1995; Olney, 1995; Sheehan & Matuozzi, 1996; Steering Committee, 1993; Weiss, Wagner, & Bauman, 1996).

Regardless of the controversy, disengaging literacy as an end-product of a rigid curriculum and recognizing its value as a tool for building relationships fostered the active membership of all students in particular classroom communities. Lee Larson, for instance, was a grade-level participant in every academic subject matter studied by the class. Shayne Robbins, who firmly believed written language should be presented to all students as communication, had her children cooperatively construct a daily community journal. Following lunch, the children gathered in small groups to describe the things they had done throughout the morning. Certain students wrote out words, others drew pictures, some scribbled; Isaac and April scribbled and scrawled designs. The children then explained their *writing*, and the stories were combined into a group journal entry written by the teacher on large paper. April signed and gestured to express her writing. Isaac pointed to written options that the teacher transferred into the journal. In this simple act, literacy as a tool for connection engaged all children at multiple levels and in an extremely natural, cooperative manner.

AN END TO ILLITERACY: DOWN SYNDROME IN THE CONTEXT OF THE LITERATE COMMUNITY

Culturally imposed illiteracy is not unique to people categorized as having Down syndrome. Devalued groups throughout history have been subjected to the circular illogic of the privileged and powerful: first separated from the literate web of community and then, when reading proved difficult, represented as lacking the intellectual capacity to engage with the written word (Resnick & Resnick, 1977). Shevin (1993) pointed out that the great American poet Phillis Wheatley (1753–1784), brought to the United States from Africa as a slave, was initially characterized by the Boston community as a fraud because it was believed no person of African heritage could create verse.

Impoverished black Americans to this day continue to face intellectual oppression similar to that experienced by Wheatley more than 200 years ago. Kozol (1991), in a powerful exploration of segregated urban schools, found horrific and savage inequalities between the education afforded the affluent upper classes and that provided to the poor and the underclass. In one partially condemned elementary school in the ghetto of Chicago's South Side, Kozol uncovered the separation of students from literacy opportunities:

> Library books, which have been piled and abandoned in the lunchroom of the school, have sprouted mold. Some years ago, the school received the standard reading textbooks out of sequence: The second workbook in the reading program came to the school before the first. The principal, uncertain what to do with the wrong workbook, was told by school officials it was, "All right to work backwards." (1991, p. 53)

The justifications given for this assault on children's intellectual opportunities, and hence their potential, tend to focus blame on the children themselves. Administrators in these districts, businesspeople in these communities, and affluent parents in nearby communities suggest that the schools merely reflect the cognitive needs and realities of the students contained therein. If they cannot demonstrate conformity to established curricula standards, so the logic goes, then they inevitably must face banishment from valued community opportunities, including literacy opportunities.

Kozol (1991) notes that this reasoning has led to an evolution of two parallel curricula, one for urban and one for suburban youth. The poor children, at extremely young ages, are written off as societal burdens locked into slots of reduced and narrowed opportunities. He recounts a Chicago businessman telling him, "It doesn't make sense to offer something that most of these urban kids will never use. No one expects these ghetto kids to go to college. Most of them are lucky if they're even literate" (p. 76).

The mass tracking of America's minority and poor children into a curriculum of lost opportunities and hopelessness parallels that experienced by segregated students with Down syndrome and other disabilities (Borthwick, 1996). These children, also charged with having the differences that matter, are siphoned into diagnostic/prescriptive instructional arrangements with functional outcome goals reflective of professional judgments as to their defectiveness and deficiency. The structures of segregated education systematically deny students virtually any opportunity to enter the literate community as valued participants. Mark Jersey, for instance, in his self-contained learning disabilities classroom, was placed at a second-grade reading level and forced to complete corresponding workbooks and worksheets filled with isolated subskill practice activities. This occurred despite the extended periods he spent silently reading motorcycle magazines written generally at a fifth-grade level. Mark's teacher, Jim McClanahan, lamented, "That's the thing. I haven't even really had a chance to sit down and hear him read or anything like that."

Jim explained that Mark's reading level was primarily ascertained from his group participation. However, group participation was hindered by ridicule Mark received from his peers due to his articulation difficulties. Jim said:

> Mark won't say anything because he's real embarrassed about the way he sounds. The kids can be real pricks about it too. Like I say, he's embarrassed. Real self-conscious about everything. So when he's in a group he's all hunched over, hiding out. Nothing else. That's how he is. He's like a turtle who's got to hide.

The peer pecking order had effectively reduced Mark's literacy status, but not without adult reinforcement. For instance, in one lesson I observed, a reading specialist, trying to hear Mark's response to a question on forming conclusions, shouted at the rest of the group, "Quiet! Even if he could answer, I couldn't hear him." Though he had previously demonstrated an ability to respond to her questions, the teacher clearly conveyed doubt as to Mark's ability.

Breaking with Tradition: A Research Base

Despite their consistent banishment to the periphery of the literate community, a growing body of often ignored research and biography documents the power of the written word in the lives of people with Down syndrome. In the 1940s, at the Bancroft School in Haddonfield, New Jersey, students with Down syndrome were recognized as extremely literate: "We have found that mongoloids are capable of attaining mental ages and intelligence quotients much higher than is generally believed possible" (Pototzky & Grigg, 1942, p. 503).

Of the 11 children with Down syndrome at the school, 2 scored at the sixth-grade reading level, 7 ranged from first-grade through fifth-grade levels, and 2 were considered prereaders (Pototzky & Grigg, 1942). Writing proved a more difficult endeavor than reading for these children: "Learning to write is always a long and tedious lane requiring perhaps three or four years. One case, male, required five years to learn to write, but constant effort by his teacher and himself brought him the *tool* which makes his life happiest" (Pototzky & Grigg, 1942, p. 509; emphasis added). Pototzky and Grigg (1942) concluded:

> We propose, therefore, that the term "Mongolian idiocy" so frequently found in the literature be discarded, and the term "Mongolism" which more accurately describes the physical and not the mental status, be substituted. (p. 510)

In the 1960s, two journals typed by people with Down syndrome were published as autobiographies (Hunt, 1966; Seagoe, 1964). Both were initially suspected to be frauds. Nigel Hunt's father, living with his family in the United Kingdom, writes in the introduction:

> We—[Nigel's] mother and I—know from experience that it will be extremely difficult to persuade anyone that this book is exactly what it professes to be. Many "experts" have preconceived ideas of what "these children" can do. They do not easily admit that they have underestimated them. (Hunt, 1966, pp. 16–17)

Seagoe, a psychologist, published Paul Scott's journal only after several publishing companies rejected her efforts based on the assumption that no person with Down syndrome could type the complex prose contained in the detailed description of Scott's everyday life.

Both Nigel Hunt and Paul Scott struggled against professional attitudes in their efforts to join the literate community, and both succeeded in their struggle only because their parents assumed the children's community citizenship and, along with it, their right to engage with the written word. Paul Scott, for instance, was brought by his father at age 7 to a well-known teacher in California, Hellen Bass Keller. Keller had taught a number of difficult students to read, but on meeting Paul she believed him to be uneducable:

> He spoke no intelligible words or sentences and asked no questions. He made incoherent sounds as he played, pulling out the drawers of her desk, taking the chalk and erasers from the blackboard and laughing with joy as he threw them at the ceiling (Seagoe, 1964, p. 12)

Keller gently explained to Paul's father that Paul would never read, but his father resisted the prognosis: "Paul can learn," he said. "He is not mentally retarded" (quoted in Seagoe, 1964, p. 12). Keller relented and engaged Paul in a dual instructional process focused on motor control and the use of written language in communicative contexts. In less than a year,

Paul was able to produce written texts conveying his thoughts. For instance, one scrawled note to Keller read, "I love you. Will see you soon. Paul." At one point during that first year, Keller brought in a typewriter for Paul to see. He was fascinated by it. Seagoe (1964) wrote, "That was the beginning of his self-taught use of the typewriter, a consuming interest and an indispensable tool" (p. 286).

At the age of 12, Paul began to keep a journal that would continue to the end of his life. His writing suggests he developed into a sophisticated and thoughtful man. In 1940, at the age of 20, Paul typed:

> October 23. after breakfast to little rock arkansas; i saw the leaves in colors of autumn; the veins in the leaves are fingerprints of god in the middle western united states; the god is almighty and thank god for america and we are out of war; christ is a rock in the weary land." (quoted in Seagoe, 1964, p. 288)

In the introduction to Nigel Hunt's (1966) book, Nigel's father described how he and his wife had always assumed Nigel would read and had provided him with daily literacy experiences that connected print to his everyday life. For instance, when he helped his mother cook or clean, she would point out labels and he would spell the words using magnetic letters. He began reading books at an early age. His father demonstrated the use of a typewriter, and Nigel quickly took to it as a tool for conveying his own thoughts. However, certain school personnel refused to believe Nigel was literate. One teacher suggested, on being shown Nigel's typed notes, that his parents had actually done the writing.

In the foreword to Hunt's (1966) book, a noted Down syndrome expert, Dr. L. S. Penrose, described the work as exciting but suggested it affirmed the "classical features" of Down syndrome: "Preoccupation with musical performance is evident. . . . He never makes a generalization . . . experiences of the same kind are not compared to one another" (p. 10). However, on reading Nigel's prose, one is forced to reconsider Penrose's interpretation. Nigel readily admits that if he had been able to choose, "I would have written the entire book just about pop music, but my dad says people will be more interested in my adventures" (Hunt, 1966, p. 289). His "preoccupation with musical performance" was an obsession with the Beatles, certainly not an abnormality for a 17-year-old living in England (or anywhere else in the world) in the mid-1960s.

In Nigel's richly descriptive prose, numerous generalizations and comparisons also appear on almost every page. For instance, he writes:

> On Cooper's Hill is the memorial to President J. F. Kennedy when he was assassinated at the hands of Lee Oswald who is now dead. . . . Since Presi-

dent Kennedy's death at Dallas, Texas I was extremely cross, well, extremely sorry. Then came the news of Sir Winston Churchill's death. The doctor came to see him, still in bed he had his hombre hat on. (Hunt, 1966, p. 65)

Hunt's book, like Paul Scott's journal, suggests a thoughtful human being whose greatest struggle was not with Down syndrome itself but with attitudes that relegated him to a devalued social place.

More recently, Buckley (1985, 1995) and Meyers (1986, 1988, 1990) have provided research documentation of the sophisticated capacities of students with Down syndrome to engage with written language for communication purposes. Buckley's interest originated with a letter she received in 1980 from a father who described his daughter with Down syndrome learning to read at the age of 3. Buckley initiated a research project with 15 preschoolers, all of whom had Down syndrome, in which she consistently discovered what appeared to be precocious literacy abilities. At extremely young ages, such as 25 months, 28 months, and 3 years and 5 months, her research participants demonstrated abilities to read and comprehend words printed on flashcards. The child who read at 25 months was unable to speak at all: "He demonstrated his comprehension by reading the flashcard and pointing to the correct object or picture" (Buckley, 1995, p. 159).

The children's reading amazed Buckley, who was also stunned by two other related discoveries. First, she found the type of reading mistakes made by the children with Down syndrome surprising. Buckley had assumed the youngsters would have the traditional dilemmas with phonetic decoding. Though this did occur, Buckley was astounded when a more consistent error pattern emerged in which the children expressed a phrase that conveyed the same meaning as the word on the flashcard, but was not that word. For instance, "a child looks at the printed word *shut* and says *closed* or looks at *sleep* and says *go to bed* (Buckley, 1995, p. 159).

Buckley (1985, 1995) suggested this meant that the word was translated directly into its meaning, and from its meaning the children chose a word or phrase to express the definition. Tradition holds that we first translate a word into its spoken sound, and then find its meaning. Thus speech has been emphasized as an indicator of one's readiness to read, which often results in the segregation of students with poor speech from literacy opportunities (see Kangas & Lloyd, 1988, for an insightful critique of the logic that keeps children who lack speech away from written language.) Buckley concluded that written language acted, in effect, as a first language for her students with Down syndrome rather than as a secondary language mediated by speech.

Secondly, Buckley (1985, 1995) discovered that reading enhanced the children's spoken language, and this was true for preschoolers as well as adolescents with Down syndrome. She noted the following observations: (1) Words read from flashcards emerge (often quickly) in children's speech; (2) reading phrases accelerates the use of spoken phrases; (3) speech grammar and syntax is improved by reading; and (4) reading improves phonology and articulation. A large body of research supports Buckley's contention that the use of print and symbols supports the development of children's speech (Beukelman & Mirenda, 1992; Garton & Pratt, 1989; Jago, Jago, & Hart, 1984; Kouri, 1989; Roch, 1978; Simons-Derr, 1983; Wolf & McAlonic, 1977).

The success Buckley experienced in using print to enhance her students' communication is reflected in the work of Meyers (1986, 1988, 1990) as well. Meyers has made extensive use of word-processing programs with computer-generated voice output to develop the expressive abilities of students with Down syndrome. She noted, "I started using computers after five frustrating years of working with children who had very little expressive ability due to Down syndrome" (1986, p. 20). Meyers discovered that many of her nonspeaking students could learn to write in grammatical sentences prior to the emergence of speech. One nonspeaking student typed at the age 13, "[God] is going to like this. I can hear God talking in my head. I like his finest whispers" (1986, p. 22).

The research suggests that children with Down syndrome are able to express sophisticated literacies when written language serves as a tool for community connectedness. Certainly Shayne Robbins and Colleen Madison's classroom experiences support this. They recognized in their students with Down syndrome a literate dimension that emerged in community participation. Based on the realization of their students' literate value, the teachers opened up opportunities to use written language to enhance classroom relationships. In doing so, the social place of their children with Down syndrome progressively evolved in a direction of value as citizens of the literate community.

6

Citizenship, Behavior, and Friendship

In the Kingsley and Levitz autobiographical account of growing up with Down syndrome, the young men's mothers, Emily P. Kingsley and Barbara G. Levitz, write in the introduction:

> Over the years, we have struggled against the prevailing philosophy that children with Down syndrome are, by definition, not educable. Many school districts believe it is inappropriate to include children with Down syndrome in regular schools or regular classes and that it is a waste of time to teach them academics. (Kingsley & Levitz, 1994, p. 5)

Emily and Barbara intuitively recognized in their children a right to belong in the wider community. They proceeded to create opportunities that would connect Jason and Mitchell to their nondisabled peers. Through "battles, struggles, defeats, and much hard work" the possibility of connection to the community was realized (Kingsley & Levitz, 1994, p. 6). Jason and Mitchell "thrived in public school." Through an ever-expanding network of friends, the two established a "tremendous sense of belonging and security. And as their confidence and abilities increased, one success built on another" (Kingsley, & Levitz, 1994, p. 6).

Forming friendships, however, was not a simple endeavor for either Jason or Mitchell. Mitchell admitted that, in high school, he resorted at times to embarrassing himself in order to receive attention from his nondisabled peers. He recalled:

> One of the immature things I did was I made up raps about women and I say out loud on the bus, going to our [soccer] games, to away games. They [his nondisabled teammates] were laughing at me when I would do this, and I felt I was being too immature. I was just doing it for fun. To get attention. (Kingsley & Levitz, 1994, p. 48)

Jason remembered how awkward it was to approach a nondisabled classmate on whom he had developed a crush. He explained, "She was in main-

stream [nondisabled]. It's very different from in special ed. It's very difficult for a special ed person to approach a mainstream person like this"
(Kingsley, & Levitz, 1994, p. 74).

Entering into relationships of mutual respect, thus opening the possibility of friendship, requires that students be recognized for their inherent
humanness and significance as symbolic beings. Van der Klift and Kunc
(1994) note that such recognition only occurs when schools work to establish a *valuing paradigm* (see Chapter 4) in which no students are officially
and categorically devalued based on interpretations of defect attached to
their nonconformity.

THE POWER OF INTERPRETATION
IN THE CONTEXT OF FRIENDSHIP

"Friendship is about choice and chemistry," Van der Klift and Kunc (1994)
remind us. "It cannot be readily defined, much less forced" Teachers, however, have the power to "create and foster an environment in which it is
possible for friendship to emerge" (p. 394). Such a context is constructed
on the underlying assumption that all children have the right to membership as citizens in classroom communities. Within the framework of citizenship, children's behavior, no matter what its appearance, is understood
to be motivated by a desire for connection with the wider community
(McGee, Menolascino, Hobbs, & Menousek, 1987).

Teachers who recognize a fundamental motivation to bond convey to
other students the message that the child with disabilities, though different in presence, is not different in spirit. Such an acknowledgment opens
possibilities for connection that might otherwise go unrealized.

Realizing that context matters when considering the possibility of relationships requires that we also recognize the potential of school personnel to create environments that impede friendship formation. Impediments
occur when certain students experience a lack of support or are misinterpreted in their effort to connect with the wider community.

Straying from Hope: Interpretive Paths Away from Friendship

On a morning visit to Joanna Sylvester's school, I followed what had
become a familiar pattern. At approximately 9:20, one of the teachers announced to the class, "Let's move to reading. Purple group, I want to see
you back here. Greens and reds, check the board to see what you need to
be doing. Mrs. Capo, why don't you take your group to the hall?" As described in Chapter 5, Joanna Sylvester and her four peers with disabilities

spent reading and language arts periods in the hall, apart from the second-grade class, listening to Mrs. Capo read stories and coloring in ditto sheets.

On this particular morning, Mrs. Capo read from an oversized book about cats. She called individual students to stand beside her and repeat words as she read. The students seated on the floor quickly lost interest. Megan, a classmate of Joanna's, leaned toward Joanna in a manner clearly meant to exlude Kisha, a tall girl seated to Megan's left. Megan whispered something into Joanna's ear. Kisha bellowed out, "Hey, what you saying? You saying something? You best not be talking about me."

Mrs. Capo looked up from the reading. She told the child standing beside her to sit and asked Kisha to take his place. Kisha sauntered forward and, with tremendous lack of interest, began repeating the words Mrs. Capo read. At one point, Mrs. Capo strayed from the text to ask Kisha directly, "What are the cats doing in the picture?" Kisha, not realizing a question was asked, automatically repeated, "What are the cats doing in the picture?"

While Kisha stood, Megan made a great show of leaning toward Joanna and whispering loudly in her ear. Kisha screamed, "Hey! You stop that! You stop that whispering." Mrs. Capo pointed to the book and said, "Everyone needs to be paying attention here." Joanna leaned toward Megan but misjudged the distance and placed her mouth in Megan's ear. Kisha screamed out, "Stop trying to kiss!" Megan hollered, "She's my friend." "We're all friends here," Mrs. Capo shouted. Kisha stomped away and lay down on the floor. Mrs. Capo said, "Kisha, I need you to be sitting up." Kisha said, "I ain't sitting till Joanna stops kissing." Mrs. Capo, trying to move on, called one of the boys up to repeat words. Kisha, recognizing an opportunity, reached out and grabbed Megan's purse. Megan, trying to ignore Kisha, did not see this, but Joanna did.

Joanna watched as Kisha stood and walked toward the stairs. Mrs. Capo kept reading. At the railing, Kisha looked back, saw Joanna watching, and dropped the purse over the edge. Joanna struggled to her feet, walked to the railing, and looked over. She turned back to the group and pointed while vocalizing several shock-filled sounds. Mrs. Capo yelled, "Joanna, what are you doing over there? Sit back down." Kisha announced to no one in particular, "I threw Megan's purse over the edge." Megan let out a shriek and ran toward the stairs. The boy standing beside Mrs. Capo ran to the railing while Megan bounded down the stairs. The group was in complete disarray, some students down the stairs, others at the railing. The book about cats laid open on the floor where Mrs. Capo had thrown it.

Eventually, Mrs. Capo collared Kisha and pushed her into the classroom. The other children began filtering back to the reading location. After several minutes without Mrs. Capo, I suggested that we finish reading the story. The children seemed agreeable. As I read, I noted with interest that when Joanna scooted near Megan, Megan aggressively pushed her away. She said, "Don't touch me, Joanna. I don't want you touching me." Megan and Joanna's connection ultimately appeared to exist solely to hurt Kisha. When that was accomplished, Megan summarily dismissed Joanna. No hint of friendship remained. In fact, Joanna appeared extremely isolated from all of her peers in the second-grade classroom.

We finished reading the cat book, and had begun reading a book about worms, when Mrs. Capo reappeared without Kisha. As she took the book from me, she said with embarrassment, "This group is the lowest. It's so hard for them to focus on anything."

No Chance for Mutual Valuing. The possibility certainly exists that Joanna's print awareness group, in a state of extreme boredom, actively recontextualized the lesson toward one of adventure and interaction. Mrs. Capo, however, clearly did not entertain the idea that her children's anarchy represented a rebellion against the meaninglessness of their school lives; she had been trained, as had I, to blame the students' behavior on their presumed deficiencies. When children are construed as burdens, their performance reinforces the logic of banishment. Every movement is read by those around the child as a declaration of defect (Mercer, 1973; Skrtic, 1995b; Sleeter, 1986). The result is a solidified image of incompetence and a deepened disconnection from the wider community (Heshusius, 1995).

When behavior automatically intensifies an adult's perception of children as defective, a student's ability to enter into and engage in relationships of respect and value further degenerates (Villa, Udis, & Thousand, 1994). Kozol (1991) notes that when we deny children meaningful educational opportunities, those students have little reason not to disrupt the lives of other students. "Knowing one is ruined," Kozol writes, "is a powerful incentive to destroy opportunities for other children" (p. 118).

However, a prominent tradition in special education insists on blaming the disenfranchised students themselves when they experience disconnection from the community. Situations like Joanna's print awareness group, what I call a squatter's position, are held up as examples of the ineffectiveness and potential danger of inclusion itself. Serafica (1990), for instance, argued that students with Down syndrome would inherently suffer isolation when grouped with nondisabled students: "It appears," he explained, "that 'like seeks out like'" (p. 378). This, he suggested, was a manifestation of children's natural inclinations toward seeking *equality*. Sinson and Wetherick (1981) agree, contending that a child with Down syndrome in an inclusive classroom will inherently become "an isolate in the group" (p. 119).

The absence of valuing relationships, however, is a consequence of representation, not of intrinsic defect (Bogdan & Taylor, 1989). When one is, by formal edict, labeled as a burden, separated, segregated, "ruined" (as described by Kozol, 1991), and ostracized, forming relationships based on value and respect is, at best, difficult. Behaviors emanating from a *ruined* child that strike out at such a representation serve only to further the logic that banished the child initially, thus widening the gap between the student and the community. Rafael Oberti's experience serves as a perfect example.

Rafael, a young child with Down syndrome, was placed in a half-day developmental kindergarten for students considered not yet ready for the rigors of the kindergarten curriculum. His access to the developmental program represented a Clementon, New Jersey, school district *compromise* with Rafael's parents, who had requested that Rafael have opportunities to interact with nondisabled children. The school district had automatically sought a fully segregated placement for Rafael. The developmental kindergarten represented middle ground.

In the developmental class, with few accommodations and little support, Rafael hit students, scratched, and hid from teachers. Based on this aggression, the school district again sought to segregate Rafael. His parents agreed to visit several segregated programs, but they found none that appeared to offer Rafael educational hope.

Eventually, however, the Obertis acquiesced to the district's pressure and enrolled Rafael in a self-contained class for children with multiple handicaps on the condition that the Clementon school district explore limited mainstreaming possibilities. The district, however, failed to move on its end of the bargain, and the Obertis filed a civil action in the United States District Court for the District of New Jersey (*Oberti v. Board of Education*, 1992). Based on lengthy testimony and video observation, the court ruled in favor of the Obertis and demanded that the Clementon school district provide appropriate supports to Rafael in a school setting that allowed meaningful engagement with nondisabled children.

On appeal by the school district, the United States Court of Appeals for the Third Circuit concurred with the lower court's ruling. In its decision, the court stated that the school district had, in effect, set Rafael up to be a behavior problem:

> The Obertis' evidence supports the district court's finding that Rafael would not have had such severe behavior problems had he been provided with adequate supplementary aids and services in that [developmental] kindergarten class, and that Rafael would most likely not present such problems if he were included in a regular class at that time. (*Oberti v. Board of Education*, 1993)

The Clementon school district's lawyer, Thomas J. Murphy, after losing the case, blasted the court of appeals in an article for the *National Review* (Murphy, 1994). He described young Rafael as a "mentally retarded 5-year-old with an IQ of 59 and a mental age of 2 who cannot speak intelligibly and who must be taken to the bathroom every 15 minutes" (Murphy, 1994, p. 56). Murphy noted that, as a 5-year-old, and with a presumed toddler's intellect, Rafael frequently "assaulted" his teachers (p. 56); he suggested that the ruling by the court of appeals "puts mentally retarded, speech-impaired, non-toilet-trained, extremely disruptive children with disparate needs in regular public school classes" (p. 56).

Both the district and appeals courts, however, saw a very different child than the one described by Murphy. The courts witnessed a little boy who readily engaged in academic lessons with his caring mother; participated successfully in groups of children, including at church school; and was developing communication skills under the thoughtful guidance of private language professionals. With appropriate and reasonable supports, both courts ruled, Rafael could and would be a valued part of a regular classroom. The disconnection Rafael experienced in his developmental kindergarten, the courts observed, led to disruptive behaviors that were then used against him to support further banishment. The courts saw through this spiraling illogic and ordered that it be stopped.

Interpreting Behavior Toward Friendship

The conclusion arrived at in the *Oberti* civil suits, recognizing Rafael's community potential if reasonably accommodated, is supported by the citizenship experiences of numerous students with Down syndrome in schools around the world (Andrews, 1995; Booth, 1985; Burke & McDaniel, 1991; Goode, 1992; Harris, 1994; Kingsley & Levitz, 1994; Luke, 1995). The evidence suggests that Rafael's behavior and Joanna Sylvester's isolation are not inherent consequences of Down syndrome but are instead cultural constructions based on their representation as a community burden.

In contrast to the school-created images of Rafael and Joanna, Lee Larson, who was nonspeaking and every bit as motorically awkward as Joanna, was considered a valued member of Colleen Madison's second grade. Certainly he experienced moments of isolation, as did every one of his classmates. And certainly Lee's moments of isolation were, at times, specifically tied to differences in communication and behavior. For instance, in Chapter 3 I described a brief separation from the wider class when Lee inadvertently ate glue. In the drama of the situation, and with Lee lacking an efficient method for explaining the circumstances, a teacher's associate had interpreted the act as volitional, and Lee was left looking mildly ridiculous. In general, however, Lee actively participated in the social patterns of the nondisabled children both in and out of school.

Friendship as a Consequence of Human Reciprocity. The acceptance Lee experienced among his peers originated with the assumption held by his teacher, Colleen Madison, that all children had a right to membership in the regular routines and normal patterns of her second-grade class. Colleen recognized in Lee's idiosyncratic behavior a desire to be understood as a thoughtful student. For instance, at the conclusion of a reading unit, Lee participated with his reading group in taking a unit test. One section of the assessment required that Colleen read questions while the children responded in a multiple-choice format. Rather than using a pencil, Lee pointed to his option, and a student teacher marked his answer.

As the test progressed, Lee became increasingly agitated and vocal. The student teacher told him several times, "Lee, you need to be quiet. You need to calm down." After several minutes, Colleen said to the group, "I think Lee wants to go faster. We'll pick up the pace, and if this is a problem for anyone, let me know. We can work out a compromise." She turned to Lee and said, "We'll work a bit faster Lee, but you know you have better ways to tell me." Colleen then picked up the pace of the test. Lee immediately relaxed and focused on his work.

Colleen could easily have dismissed Lee's behavior as simple noncompliance. However, in her interpretation of his communicative intent, Colleen conveyed to both Lee and his classmates that Lee's behavior was a unique, albeit not entirely appropriate, expression of competence. Colleen told me later:

> See, I think we're at [Lee's] ceiling in terms of him being at a real comfortable level. A lot of the other kids are actually going too slow for him. He gets frustrated. That's the feeling I get. Yeah, so we let him work ahead, and make sure he's ready when it's his turn to be called on.

This image of Lee as a thoughtful being appeared to carry over to his classmate's interpretations of his behavior. For instance, one afternoon after completing an assignment early, Lee was allowed some free time. He retrieved a container of Lincoln Logs and began stacking them in a corner of the room. When he had a small structure built, Lee brought his foot down, smashing it into pieces. A classmate joined him and took a more organized approach to the building, laying out a square foundation. He said to Lee, "Now you put the next logs on." Lee added a layer, and his classmate added the next layer, alternating until they had a fairly tall structure built. After a roof was added, the two simultaneously smashed it, which led to shrieks of laughter from both boys. A third child joined the two, but when the next structure neared completion, Leah George, a classroom assistant, appeared, and said, "I hope you're not planning on doing anything that might get you in trouble." Lee smiled at Leah, but the building remained standing. The three boys turned their energies to constructing a series of buildings, with Lee adding logs after the foundations were laid out.

The boys' play appears mundane—a scene acted out in countless classrooms across the country when children gather together enjoying one another's company (often at the expense of classroom rules). However, the normality of the situation involving a child who, just 2 years previously, had been considered severely mentally retarded is what makes it noteworthy. In Colleen's classroom, Lee's actions with the Lincoln Logs, though construed as misbehavior, were not considered deviant per se. They represented any child's love for destroying things, and his peers joined in with gusto. Lee had, in effect, taken on a valued leadership role, with friends rallying to him. In reimposing the classroom rules, Leah addressed the children's behavior with the recognition that each, including Lee, knew better than to smash Lincoln Logs.

The Importance of Connection. On initially entering Colleen's class, Lee had been disconnected from his peers (see Chapters 4 and 5). The teachers did not yet know how to understand him, and he had no systematic way for communicating his thoughts. He had been aggressive in his behavior, scratching and biting to make his points, and he actively separated himself from others in the class. Often, this took the form of running away. Colleen remembered:

> The kids would be walking in a line to art or somewhere, and suddenly, Lee would bolt. He'd be gone. We couldn't find him. He'd have this agenda. He wanted to be away. One time, he didn't even come into school until about 10:30. I don't know if you heard about that incident? I still haven't recovered. I was beside myself. I still wonder where he spent that morning.

Colleen's intuitive sense of Lee's citizenship, however, led her away from interpreting his behavior as defective. Rather, she saw in his actions an available form of expression that conveyed resistance to a context that was not yet responsive to Lee's unique needs. Colleen explained:

> I really think teaching is problem solving. That you deal. And that's what you model to kids because that's what learning is: working

through problems. There's always more than one way. That's what we try to model for our kids.

As described in Chapters 4 and 5 and above, the teaching staff and support personnel initiated a concerted effort to construct supports for Lee's curricular and communicative participation. Consequently, his aggressive and fleeing behaviors diminished. By the second month of school, he no longer escaped the class at all and he rarely lashed out at friends.

The connections Lee formed in class then carried over to the community. He was invited to birthday parties, after-school activities, sleep-overs, and other normal childhood events. His mother told me, "Lee's social life is unreal. I feel like his secretary. His brothers aren't invited to half what he gets invited to."

Isaac Johnson, like Lee Larson, also found a central place in the patterns of friendship in Shayne Robbins's classroom. Despite Isaac's unconventional modes of communication and ostensibly difficult-to-decipher behaviors, he was accepted by friends as an important part of the preschool community's web of relationships.

Isaac's best friend was a nondisabled classmate, Dan, who shared with Isaac a love for books. The two attached themselves to one another each morning and were rarely separated throughout the school day. In the library section of the room, they would page through books pointing, laughing, and jabbering together. They would move together to the classroom's wooden block area and join other children in constructing towns populated by Fisher-Price Little People. At circle time the two had spots located next to each other and would sit holding hands as the day's events were discussed.

Shayne felt that the boys' close friendship originated with their mutual interest in literature. "A lot of what they talk about, do together," Shayne explained, "is book-related. Dan is another kid who is incredible in his literacy. They really play the books they love." Isaac's lack of speech did not serve as an obstacle to their mutual enjoyment of one another. Shayne noted:

It's interesting when you watch them communicate, and Isaac will tell one of his stories and you have no idea what he just said, and Dan responds like he knows exactly what was just said. And then Dan will take his turn with the conversation, and he'll talk about something. And they have these amazing conversations that any adult looking at it would only get Dan's part of it, and yet Dan is real content with Isaac's participation. They have these incredible conversations.

As Shayne alluded to, Dan's lack of concern with Isaac's communicative nonconformity might strike certain adults as bizarre. However, Isaac and Dan's relationship formed within a context that recognized Isaac as inherently valuable and that supported Isaac's participation as a rightful citizen of the community. This teacher-established framework for understanding and interpreting children clearly carried over to the students. They rarely, if ever, were observed distinguishing one another based on traditional adult-imposed structures of banishment that charge only certain students with having the differences that matter.

COMMUNITY AND FRIENDSHIP

Lee Larson's and Isaac Johnson's capacity to enter friendships reinforces what has previously been demonstrated in the context of human development generally (Chapter 4) and literacy and communication development specifically (Chapter 5): Citizenship is fundamental to perceptions of competence; connectedness is central to the recognition of valued human reciprocity. Segregation from democratic participation, whether it occurs in schools or the wider community, destroys opportunities to enter mutually valuing relationships.

Both John Mcgough's (Andrews, 1995) and Christine Durovich's (Harris, 1994) life experiences further illustrate the importance of social place in the context of friendship formation. John (as described in Chapter 4) spent his high school years defined as uneducable, segregated into a self-contained school, and isolated from the community. He had no friends apart from his family. After leaving school and moving to Mendocino, California, where he was accepted by the townspeople as a worthwhile individual, John's social network dramatically expanded. At a birthday party given in his honor and attended by 200 residents, John told the celebrants, "I just want you to know, thanks a lot . . . and I feel my love, deep in me, for the people who I see right now" (quoted in Andrews, 1995, p. 111).

In explaining the contrast between the numbers of friends he enjoyed in Mendocino compared to his former life of isolation, John told Andrews (1995), "Some people gotta pop out of some attitudes and problems" (p. 115). John's brother said, "People will look at John and expect a certain thing to happen, and that thing won't happen. Something else will happen that does not fit their preconceived notions of what John should be doing or being, and then they'll be, in effect, popped out" (p. 115). According to John, his segregated schooling had not allowed people around him to "pop out" of their devaluing "attitudes and problems." After escaping the segregated context and entering into the regular routines of community life in Mendocino, John was able to enter into the patterns of friendship that exist as possibilities when one is recognized as a valuable human being.

As with John, Christine Durovich's segregated education up to the age 14 had resulted in her community isolation. She responded to her exclusion with what Harris (1994) described as "behavioral challenges" and "acting-out behaviors" (pp. 294, 295). Her entry as a freshman into a regular high school and general education curriculum had profound consequences for Christine and the wider community. For instance, the perceptions of people around Christine regarding her academic capacities were dramatically altered following her inclusion (Harris, 1994; see Chapters 4 and 5). After graduating from high school, she enrolled in Trinity College, where she studied until her untimely death at age 21 following a brief illness.

In conjunction with the realization of her academic competence, Christine's social network expanded in a manner similar to John Mcgough's after he left behind his segregated education. Her freshman year position on the cheerleading squad had connected her to a peer group that, in turn, helped her to meet and form bonds with more and more students throughout the school. The following year, Christine's role on the school paper provided her with a new opportunity to develop friendships while her weekly newspaper column enhanced her valued social place. As her academic and social capacities were realized, the aggression that had characterized Christine's behavior in her segregated school diminished to a point of nonexistence (Harris, 1994).

The logic that initially forced John and Christine into a segregated realm was ostensibly cloaked in good intentions. It suggests that they and others perceived to be like them are so defective that specially trained educators must first remediate the children's behavior and then, once remediated, the children can access nonsecluded, nonspecialized environments with the potential to perhaps form friendships. Segregated remediation, so goes the logic, has the capacity to focus specifically on the development of social skills. Success with individualized friendship goals in segregated schools is thought to establish the conditions for friendship formation beyond the walls of the self-contained classroom. There is, however, a distinct lack of data supporting this claim (see, for instance, Lipsky & Gartner's [1989] thoughtful and ultimately futile search for evidence upholding segregationist logic).

As John, Christine, Lee Larson, and Isaac Johnson demonstrate, acceptance is based on the condition of acceptance itself. The precursors to friendship and the behaviors associated with mutually valuing relationships are not found in the behavioral checklists hung like operant-inspired art on the walls of segregated classrooms but are instead located in one's community membership, citizenship, and democratic participation. When a student's experiences, no matter how idiosyncratic, join with the web of relationships that form the wider community, the terrain is then established on which one's human capacities and potential to form friendships can be realized.

7

The Reconceptualization
of Down Syndrome

Sandra Jensen was first introduced in Chapter 1 struggling with segments of the California medical establishment over her right to be placed on an organ candidate waiting list. Personnel at the Stanford University Medical Center and the University of California at San Diego Medical Center initially turned her candidacy down, ostensibly based on the presumption that Sandra, having Down syndrome, "lacked the intelligence to follow the complex recovery regime of pills, doctor visits, and exercise" (Wilson, 1997, p. A19).

Disability rights activists, however, including Sandra herself, recognized in the de facto death sentence a value judgment suggesting Sandra's life was worth less than that of a nondisabled American (Goldberg, 1996). Sandra explained, "I just wanted to be treated like everybody else" (quoted in Wilson, 1997, p. A19). She wished to live in order to pursue her interest in art, swimming, and advocacy work. She did eventually receive the multiple-organ transplant, but only after months of concerted battles that involved legal maneuvers invoking the nondiscriminatory mandate of the Americans with Disabilities Act (Public Law 101-336, 1990), a national advocacy campaign in support of Sandra, and Sandra's diligent efforts on her own behalf despite her failing respiratory system.

Following the successful operation, and before eventually succumbing to lymphoma, Sandra renewed her commitment to the struggle for equal constitutional protection of all people with disabilities. Her medical victory, she realized, must ultimately be tied to the larger democratic movement that seeks to end the image of community burden attached to Down syndrome and disability and build in its place a realization of human possibility. Sandra explained, "I want to be in control of my own life. I want to show others what people can do despite their disability" (quoted in Goldberg, 1996, p. 22).

To that end, Sandra lectured nationally on the right to community access and full democratic participation for all people (Jensen, 1996). She also continued an effort begun prior to the operation, visiting public schools to speak with students on the importance of respecting and valuing peers with disabilities. Sandra's school visits brought her into classrooms that she, as a student, had been barred from entering years earlier. As an adult, she was no longer forced to confront school segregation, yet she chose to do so because she realized that attitudes toward disability could not be transformed without a fundamental shift in school culture.

TOWARD SCHOOL CITIZENSHIP

Sandra Jensen's story, and the stories throughout this book of student, teacher, and family efforts to achieve school citizenship for people with Down syndrome, should not be misconstrued as isolated testimonials to the power of the individual to overcome great obstacles in lonely pursuit of social justice. Rather, they are stories that can only be understood when joined together. Each is a part of a wider struggle-in-progress transforming schools in a quest for community membership.

From the stories told, several important themes emerge that allow us to better understand the reconceptualization of Down syndrome from an image of school burden to one of citizen. These themes include the following:

1. It is necessary to acknowledge that school banishment to the status of alien or squatter is a *moral decision* based on an individual's cultural devaluation.
2. Community acceptance is fundamental to the realization of human reciprocity.
3. Acceptance into the school community as a full participant is necessary in order that an individual reach her or his educational potentials.
4. Individual language and communication capacities can only be realized on the terrain of community.
5. Friendship is a potential consequence of community connection.

I will briefly revisit each of the points.

Banishment Is a Moral Decision Based on an Individual's Cultural Devaluation

Currently, relegating students with Down syndrome to the status of alien and squatter is cloaked in the language of the medical and natural sciences. Segregation is considered a *best practice* built on the science of disability.

More than a half-century of school research, however, has resulted in no data supporting the effectiveness of segregation in teaching students to become a valued part of the community (Blatt, 1956, 1966; Booth, 1985; Buck, 1955; Butterfield, 1961; Dunn, 1968; Hunt, 1966; Knoblock, 1982; Lipsky & Gartner, 1989; Sarason, 1959; Sobsey & Dreimanis, 1993; Taylor, 1988; Vygotsky, 1930–1935/1978, 1993). Dr. Lou Brown, professor of education at the University of Wisconsin, Madison, acting as an expert witness in the *Oberti v. Board of Education* suit (see Chapter 6), pointed out that in seeking to segregate young Rafael

> [the school district] seems to be saying that in order to have success in an integrated society, Rafael first must demonstrate success in one that is segregated. Success in special schools and special classes does not lead to successful functioning in an integrated society. There is no evidence that success in segregated placements can be transferred and much evidence that teaching skills and behaviors in segregated settings is counterproductive to success in integrated settings. (*Oberti v. Board of Education*, 1992, pp. 5–6)

The dearth of data supporting segregation points to a single fundamental conclusion: Banishment to educational realms apart from the mainstream is not reflective of science. It is instead a moral decision made by people in positions of authority based on the cultural devaluation of particular individuals and groups of people charged with having the differences that matter.

Community Acceptance Is Fundamental to the Realization of Human Reciprocity

The stigma attached to Down syndrome is a consequence of the cultural inference that individuals with Down syndrome lack intellect and, hence, social utility. Categorizing particular human beings as useless, however, is a social construction that has nothing to do with their intrinsic human capacities. Singham (1995) pointed out that throughout the twentieth century, the image of the contributing, cognizant citizen has consistently taken on the appearance of the socially privileged and powerful. He noted that the established classes have "'proved' that whichever group was dominant in society at the time was dominant because of high intelligence" (p. 275). Singham reminds us:

> In the U.S. in the 1920s, there were detailed studies that "showed" that Jews and Slavic groups (who happened to be recent immigrants) were of lower intelligence than the Nordic groups who were already established here. No such claims are made today. (p. 275)

The effort to educate all children together does not seek to prove we all share equally in the multiple intellectual capacities unique to human beings. Rather, its intent is to alter the metaphor of community in order that each individual might be recognized as a rightful participant no matter what his or her strengths are in conceptualizing and acting on the universe. Instead of imagining community as a privileged location within circled wagons configured to keep out the "intellectual have-nots" (Kanner, 1942; see Chapter 1), community is reconceptualized as a web of relationships that shifts and extends to encompass the experiences of all its members. The strength of the web is in its rich diversity and recognition that each individual's contribution to the community is valuable.

Acceptance into the School Community as a Full Participant Is Necessary in Order to Meet One's Education Potential

The school community, like the wider community, is made up of relationships. In school, these relationships connect students, teachers, and materials with one another in constantly changing directions. Traditionally, students with Down syndrome have been segregation from opportunities to enter the relationships of the general school based on the image of defectiveness attached to their manner of connecting with peers, adults, and schoolwork. Segregation, its supporters contend, allows for remediation of the performance of students with Down syndrome, thus establishing the conditions for possible future acceptance into the relationships that make up the wider school community. As we have seen, however, segregation leads only to hopelessness and the need for further segregation (Sobsey & Dreimanis, 1993).

The moral framework of human reciprocity realizes that the act of learning is constructed first and foremost on a student's entry into relationships with peers, teachers, and materials. From that initial connection, all students are guided by peers, teachers, and content toward relationships of enhanced cultural value. As students' performances evolve, they, in turn, exert influence on cultural perceptions of what constitutes community value. For example, the student who successfully navigates cyberspace (a skill of questionable intrinsic utility) might today be viewed as highly valuable, while yesterday he or she might have been, and often was, stigmatized by both peers and teachers as a social misfit. In turn, more students and teachers seek the capacity to "surf the Net," and it has become an integral part of many children's schooling.

Similarly, in order that students with Down syndrome emerge from their traditional relegation to the category of misfit, they must be afforded opportunities to enter the relationships that make up the educational community. Only after their experiences are acknowledged as a strand of the web can they negotiate and reformulate their relationships toward an increasingly valued social place. In doing so, they transform and broaden the meaning of who and what is culturally valuable.

Individual Language and Communication Capacities Can Only Be Realized on the Terrain of Community

The logic of segregation contends that language must precede community participation. In the disability sciences, this has generally meant isolating children presumed to be language-deficient from nondisabled peers until remediation results in some degree of *speech* conformity. This bizarre practice emanates from the metaphor of language as an intrinsic possession of an individual: in essence, a developmental commodity measured by one's ability to speak (see Solsken, 1993, for a critical description of this myth; see also Kangas & Lloyd, 1988). Students, it is thought, must *acquire* a particular amount of language before they can enter the relationships that make up the community. An individual, however, rarely sheds the label of "language-disordered" when isolated from meaningful communicative opportunities (Kangas & Lloyd, 1988).

In contrast to segregationist logic, educating all children together realizes what Vygotsky (1930–1935/1978) first described 70 years ago: A child's systematic use of shared symbols for expressive purposes is a consequence of community participation; it is not a prerequisite to citizenship. Communication through language develops in the act of constructing meaning with others who share particular contexts. It requires that all children be acknowledged as valued human beings and as individuals motivated to join the community in a valued role. Once realized, opportunities are opened to continuously formulate and reformulate relationships in a direction of shared understanding.

Speech has traditionally served as the benchmark of a student's language capacity. However, for students with Down syndrome who struggle with speech, alternative communication methods involving multiple language literacies have proven effective. Idiosyncratic expressions are not misinterpreted as manifestations of defect but rather serve as the initial point of connection that can then be guided toward shared patterns for constructing meaning. Teachers who are able to see beyond speech difficulties into the symbolic capacities of children with Down syndrome support the children's expression through signs, symbols, and print. Language supports and accommodations must necessarily occur in meaningful contexts where children are listened to and their communicative presence is respected.

Friendship Is a Potential Consequence of Community Connection

Isolation from friendships is not a natural consequence of a trisomy at the 21st chromosome. It is, instead, the result of cultural devaluation imposed on students with Down syndrome whose socially construed defectiveness is then blamed for their lack of friendships. When students respond to their stigmatization by lashing out at those who dismiss them, their behavior is interpreted as further evidence of impairment, and the logic of banishment is reinforced.

In contrast, recognition of students with Down syndrome as rightful citizens in a framework of human reciprocity leads to the interpretation of all behavior as an effort to connect with the school community. When one's citizenship is established, idiosyncratic performance is no longer misinterpreted as a sign of deficiency and just cause for segregation; instead it is understood to be a negotiation effort toward building relationships.

As with a child's literacy development, teachers support and guide the continuous renegotiation of relationships in a direction of mutual understanding. As children learn to construct meaning together on the foundation of community, mutually valuing relationships become a very real possibility.

REALIZING THE RIGHT TO COMMUNITY MEMBERSHIP FOR STUDENTS WITH DOWN SYNDROME: A CALL FOR THE ELIMINATION OF SEGREGATED OPTIONS

In order that the above themes be realized in the actual lives of children with Down syndrome, systemic changes must occur in the general processes of schooling. Importantly, segregated classrooms (locations that exist based on the presumption of student defect) must be eliminated as an educational option for children clinically defined as mentally retarded. In conjunction with the elimination of segregated schooling, the structure of the general education classroom must change to resemble the responsive and thoughtful classrooms described in Chapters 4, 5, and 6. Will such alterations ultimately transform our cultural interpretation of disability and, indeed, our shared definition of who and what constitute valued membership in the community? Though the answer is unclear, Sandra Jensen firmly believed they would, and her spirit is joined by a number of educators, families, and scholars who suggest schools hold the potential for citizenship for all children (Dewey, 1916; Soltis, 1993; Vargo & Vargo, 1995; Villa & Thousand, 1995).

Ending Segregation

In the three preceding chapters, stories were presented of schools structured so that no child was categorically or deterministically segregated from opportunities to learn with nondisabled peers. Teachers and administrators in these schools recognized it as their responsibility to support all students' citizenship and to foster individual and group strengths within the general community of peers. However, when segregated structures exist as educational options, the question of who is responsible for children's learning becomes a muddled one. Skrtic (1995b), for instance, described special education as a bureaucratic arrangement of convenience for the removal of disorderly elements in the classroom. When faced with a nonconformist learner, one who falls outside school-set parameters of normality, teachers and administrators who rely on segregation are not forced to confront their own instructional arrangements; they simply remove the child in question as a manifestation of defect. The responsibility of instruction shifts to others. Skrtic (1995b) notes:

> The problem in the profession of education generally is that the functionalist distortion of school failure as student disability eliminates it as an anomaly and thus as an opportunity to call the prevailing (school) knowledge traditions into question. Ultimately, this prevents the profession of education (and the public) from seeing that schooling in America is inconsistent with the democratic ideals upon which public education's claim to legitimacy is premised. (p. 70)

We can begin to uncover, or perhaps create for the first time, the democratic premises of which Skrtic writes, but in order to do so, the *bureaucracy of segregation* must end.

As described in Chapter 2, federal laws emanating from the 1975 mandate that all students with disabilities receive a free and appropriate education do not recognize the terms *inclusion* or *mainstreaming*. Instead, it is decreed that "to the maximum extent appropriate" students with and without disabilities be educated together.

Although its spirit clearly values inclusive learning, the law invokes the principle of the least restrictive environment (LRE), suggesting that professionals with clinical expertise can assess a child's *condition* and then make decisions as to whether that child would achieve best in a segregated or inclusive classroom. Hence, the LRE principle actually works to legitimate segregation of individuals clinically judged to be *community burdens* (see Taylor, 1988, for a critical analysis of the LRE principle).

Research, including this study, has consistently dismantled the dual belief that (1) decisions made to segregate particular children are in any way scientifically or objectively derived (D. Biklen, 1988, 1992; Skrtic, 1995a; Taylor, 1988; Chapters 2 and 3, this volume) and (2) any child actually benefits from segregated schooling (Lipsky & Gartner, 1989). Yet the LRE principle continues to be applied in ways that maintain educational segregation as a prominent option for children with disabilities (ARC, 1995).

The challenge is clear. Schools must be reorganized to eliminate the possibility of certain children being segregated because of presumed deficiencies. This would eliminate the functionalist safety valve that is segregated education and force educators to confront practices that in effect create defect and reduce the community value of certain children.

Ending exclusionary school practices requires a transformation in policies supporting teachers and children. Funds that now go to the maintenance of the segregation bureaucracy must instead be directed toward the creation of thoughtful and supportive classrooms for all children. In many states, for instance, money slated for special education is funneled to established segregated programs rather than to individual students based on documented needs. Vast resources then go to supporting separate transportation systems, separate district and school administrations, separate physical facilities, separate teaching structures, and separate curricular programs. Children with disabilities, far from being recognized as individuals with unique needs and dreams, are fit like cogs into whatever segregated machinery preexists their entrance into special education. School segregation is indeed what Blatt (1987) referred to as a monolithic industry.

Such a system makes it difficult to financially support children with disabilities who are schooled outside the established segregated programs. Vermont, however, has devised an effective funding system whereby the money necessary to support a particular child's unique educational needs and goals follows that actual child into his or her classroom (Villa & Thousand, 1995). The result has been twofold: (1) The financial incentive to perpetuate segregation has ended, since schools receive the necessary funding to create individually responsive and thoughtful inclusive classrooms; and (2) the number of Vermont children defined as disabled placed in segregated classrooms has dramatically decreased. In a 1995 report on the percentage of students defined as mentally retarded attending inclusive schools, Vermont ranked first in the nation (ARC, 1995; see Chapter 2).

Transforming the Structure of the General Education Classroom

Does ending segregation as an option mean, then, the implementation of a single curriculum so watered down all children would fit? Absolutely not!

The merger of what have come to be called special and regular education reflects what many schools have already enacted, a sense of shared classroom and community activities as locations for *multiple educations* (Logan et al., 1994/1995; Vargo & Vargo, 1995).

The call for such an educational restructuring has indeed been strongest apart from any discussion of disability. Goodlad (1983), for instance, expressed extreme dismay at the general state of the American school. In his observations of more than a thousand schools, he encountered class after class taught primarily through lecture and whole-group instruction with minimal child–teacher interaction. He noted a distinct and systemic lack of passion for learning and teaching in the classrooms he encountered. Similarly, the Paideia Group, made up of educators from across the United States, decried the public school system's overuse of didactic instruction, lectures, and textbooks, with little consideration given to engaged, student-directed learning and critical discussion (Adler, 1982). No child, disabled or not, achieves to capacity in a static, stagnating learning environment directed not by student curiosity but by textbook publishers and traditions of efficiency.

In contrast, a classroom that recognizes the value of *multiple educations* provides all children with opportunities to participate in certain important activities but with differentiated learning goals, referred to as multilevel learning (Udvari-Solner, 1995); this is perhaps better envisioned as *array learning*, since the image of *levels* imposes a false hierarchy of value on children's experiences. Isaac Johnson, who inspired his teacher Shayne Robbins and his classmates to create the play based on *Where the Wild Things Are* (see Chapter 4), was a full participant in the production, but with goals distinct to his needs. Having already recognized him as a *reader* (i.e., able to garner information from the printed word), teachers instead focused attention on Isaac's developing ability to communicate his role to the audience in an understandable fashion using body language, sign language, and other shared patterns of expression. Certain of his classmates, more adept at communicating ideas, focused with adult support on emergent literacy goals included in the development of the play's script.

In a shared environment structured on the principle of *multiple educations*, particular activities might be shared by only some class members based on interest, curiosity, and intrigue—not perceptions of defect (Sapon-Shevin, Ayres, & Duncan, 1994). In Christine Durovich's story (Harris, 1994), for instance, participation on the high school newspaper was not required of any of the students in the school. The paper's staff was made up of students who chose to take a certain journalism class. At times of the day when classes offered did not appear to correspond to Christine's goals, she participated in a community vocational program.

In responsive classrooms, intensified instruction around certain areas of need or focus occurs without building dehumanizing walls between children (Falvey, Givner, & Kimm, 1996). Lee Larson's interest in computers, for instance, led his speech and language therapist to incorporate the classroom computer into their therapy time. One to two classmates would join Lee at the computer, providing him with opportunities to express, take turns, cooperate, argue, and engage in meaningful academic and social learning experiences while at the same time improving his communication abilities.

"Schools that work," explained Allington (1996) in a keynote address at the annual conference of the Center for Literacy and Disability Studies, "are nothing more than a set of supported and responsive classrooms." To create such classrooms requires a collaborative effort on the part of all people concerned with a particular child's education. Cunningham and Allington (1994) note that eliminating special segregated programs, "things that we know do not work" (p. 252), would bring special teachers into regular classrooms as educational collaborators, thus reducing student–teacher ratios and class sizes. They observe that in certain American schools, "we have seen that class size could be cut as low as 12–15 students" (p. 252). Collaboration also results in

> members of teaching teams bring[ing] their unique instructional expertise, areas of curriculum background, and personal interests together to provide a richer learning experience for all students. Other results are a higher teacher/student ratio, enhanced problem solving capacity, and more immediate and accurate diagnosis of student needs and delivery of appropriate instruction. (Thousand & Villa, 1995, 72)

Shayne Robbins was part of an instructional team that, as she described it, included her associates, student teachers, administrative support personnel, a psychologist, therapists, families, and the students in her class. Colleen Madison was part of a similar team, but added to it was an *inclusion coordinator*, an experienced teacher who consulted with each class in the school. Core members of the group met weekly, and each was responsible for regularly visiting the homes of children with disabilities and, albeit less often, those of the nondisabled children.

In order that collaborative efforts fulfill their potential to create thoughtful and responsive schools, administrators must assure that team teaching is a part of the school structure. For teams to work, time must be provided for meeting, planning, and problem solving. Creative use of time has included, for instance, administrators actually taking on the responsibility of teaching a class in order that members of the teaching team might meet weekly (Cunningham & Allington, 1994). At the Shoshone School, children were dismissed early every Wednesday afternoon, thus freeing up time to meet and conduct in-services. The Waterloo, Iowa, school district has recently gone to an early dismissal structure that frees up weekly planning time while concurrently increasing the amount of actual classroom time high school students spend receiving instruction (Stanton, 1997).

School personnel that have restructured to eliminate segregation as an option while creating thoughtful and supported classrooms have consistently reported sustained or improved academic achievement on the part of nondisabled students (e.g., Bear, Cleaver, & Proctor, 1991; L. Brown, 1995; Fulton, LeRoy, Pinckney, & Weekly, 1994; Hamre-Nietupski, Hendrickson, Nietupski, & Shokoohi-Yekta, 1994; Hollowood, Salisbury, Rainforth, & Palombaro, 1995; Hunt, Staub, Alwell, & Goetz, 1994; Kamps, Leonard, Potucek, & Garrison-Harrell, 1995; Pugach & Wesson, 1995). Hollowood and colleagues (1995) reported that the academic performance of nondisabled students in inclusive classrooms was equal to that of their counterparts in noninclusive arrangements and that all the students in inclusive classrooms had more extensive one-on-one interaction with teachers. L. Brown (1995) reported on a study conducted in Madison, Wisconsin, in which academic achievement of nondisabled students in inclusive classrooms was compared to achievement of students in noninclusive classrooms; again, no difference in achievement was found. Kamps and colleagues (1995) found improved reading achievement on the part of nondisabled third- and fifth-grade students in classrooms that included children with autism.

Research on schools that merge special and regular education also has documented a number of other student benefits derived from ending segregation. As outlined by Staub and Peck (1994/1995), these benefits include, among many others, an enhanced acceptance of human diversity, the development of real friendships between children with and without disabilities, and the development of personal principles consistent with democratic values (e.g., reduced tolerance of prejudice, increased responsiveness to the needs of others).

A dilemma exists with presenting a growing body of research studies documenting in overwhelming fashion the educational benefits derived for all children when segregation ends. Arguments in support of inclusive and restructured schooling begin to take on the appearance of an objectively derived *truth*. That is not my purpose at all. Calls for the elimination of segregation, or those in support of continued segregation, are not based on objective science. Instead they are guided by a moral question: What do we wish our community to look like? Though the effectiveness of schooling children with Down syndrome and other disabilities together with their nondisabled peers may in part be documented through science, its truth is instead found in the moral framework of human reciprocity that recognizes as valuable the experiences and possibilities of Lee Larson, Isaac Johnson, Joanna Sylvester, Mark Jersey, and other students described in this book. Segregation destroys our humanness. Community connection is indeed the only terrain on which our human possibility can ever be realized.

References

Abrahamsen, A. A., Romski, M. A., & Sevak, R. A. (1989). Concomitants of success in acquiring an augmentative communication system: Changes in attention, communication, and sociability. *American Journal on Mental Retardation, 93*(5), 475–496.

Adams, M. J. (1990). *Beginning to read: Thinking and learning about print.* Cambridge, MA: MIT Press.

Adler, M. J. (1982). *The Paideia proposal: An educational manifesto.* New York: Macmillan.

Allington, R. L. (1996, January). *Classrooms that work: They can ALL read and write.* Keynote presentation at the 5th Symposium on Literacy and Developmental Disabilities, Center for Literacy and Disability Studies, Durham, NC.

American Psychiatric Association (APA). (1942). Euthanasia. [Commentary]. *American Journal of Psychiatry, 99,* 141–143.

American Psychiatric Association. (1994). *Diagnostic and statistical manual of mental disorders* (4th ed.). Washington, D.C.: Author.

Andrews, S. S. (1995). Life in Mendocino: A young man with Down syndrome in a northern California town. In S. J. Taylor, R. Bogdan, & Z. M. Lutfiyya (Eds.), *The variety of community experience: Qualitative studies of family and community life* (pp. 101–116). Baltimore: Brookes.

Anwar, F., & Hermelin, B. (1979). Kinaesthetic movement after-effects in children with Down's syndrome. *Journal of Mental Deficiency Research, 23,* 287–297.

ARC (1995, August). *Report card to the nation on inclusion in education of students with mental retardation.* Arlington, TX: Author.

Ashton-Warner, S. (1963). *Teacher.* New York: Simon & Schuster.

Bacon, F. (1952). *Advancement of learning, Novum organum, New Atlantis.* Chicago: Encyclopaedia Britannica. (Original works published 1605, 1620, & 1627)

Baer, D. M., Wolf, M. M., & Risley, T. R. (1968). Some current dimensions of applied behavior analysis. *Journal of Applied Behavior Analysis, 1,* 91–97.

Baer, D. M., Wolf, M. M., & Risley, T. R. (1987). Some still-current dimensions of applied behavior analysis. *Journal of Applied Behavior Analysis, 20,* 313–327.

Baines, L. (1997). Future schlock: Using fabricated data and politically correct platitudes in the name of education reform. *Phi Delta Kappan, 79,* 493–499.

Ballard, L. (1995, January 22). Dawn's ambition: What role should college play for a woman with Down syndrome? *The Waterloo/Cedar Falls (Iowa) Courier,* pp. A1, A7.

Bear, G. G., Cleaver, A., & Proctor, W. A. (1991). Self-perceptions of nonhandi-
capped children and children with learning disabilities in integrated classes.
Journal of Special Education, 24, 409–426.

Bellah, R. N., Madsen, R., Sullivan, W. M., Swidler, A., & Tipton, S. M. (1985). *Habits
of the heart: Individualism and commitment in American life.* Berkeley: University of California Press.

Benda, C. E. (1949). *Mongolism and cretinism* (2nd ed.). New York: Grune & Stratton.

Benda, C. E. (1960). *The child with mongolism: Congenital acromicria.* New York:
Grune & Stratton.

Berkson, G., & Landesman-Dwyer, S. (1977). Behavioral research on severe and
profound mental retardation (1955–1974). *American Journal of Mental Deficiency, 81*(5), 428–454.

Bérubé, M. (1996). *Life as we know it: A father, a family, and an exceptional child.* New
York: Pantheon.

Beukelman, D. R., & Mirenda, P. (1992). *Augmentative and alternative communication: Management of severe communication disorders in children and adults.* Baltimore: Brookes.

Biklen, D. (1977). *The elementary school administrator's practical guide to mainstreaming.*
Syracuse, NY: Human Policy Press.

Biklen, D. (1983). *Community organizing: Theory and practice.* Englewood Cliffs, NJ:
Prentice-Hall.

Biklen, D. (1985). *Achieving the complete school.* New York: Teachers College Press.

Biklen, D. (1988). The myth of clinical judgment. *Journal of Social Issues, 44*(1),
127–140.

Biklen, D. (1992). *Schooling without labels: Parents, educators, and inclusive education.*
Philadelphia: Temple University Press.

Biklen, D. (1993). *Communication unbound: How facilitated communication is challeng-
ing traditional views of autism and ability/disability.* New York: Teachers College Press.

Biklen, D., & Cardinal, D. N. (Eds.). (1997). *Contested words, contested science: Un-
raveling the facilitated communication controversy.* New York: Teachers College
Press.

Biklen, S. K. (1995). *School work: Gender and the cultural construction of teaching.* New
York: Teachers College Press.

Blatt, B. (1956). *The physical, personality, and academic status of children who are mentally retarded attending special classes as compared with children who are mentally
retarded attending regular classes.* Unpublished doctoral dissertation, Pennsylvania State University, University Park.

Blatt, B. (1960). Some persistently recurring assumptions concerning the mentally
subnormal. *The Training School Bulletin, 57,* 48–59.

Blatt, B. (1966). *Intellectually disenfranchised: Impoverished learners and their teachers.*
Boston: Commonwealth of Massachusetts, Division of Mental Hygiene.

Blatt, B. (1987). *The conquest of mental retardation.* Austin, TX: Pro-Ed.

Blatt, B., Biklen, D., & Bogdan, R. (Eds.). (1977). *An alternative textbook in special
education.* Denver: Love.

Blatt, B., & Kaplan, F. (1966). *Christmas in purgatory: A photographic essay on mental retardation.* Boston: Allyn & Bacon.

Bogdan, R., & Biklen, S. K. (1992). *Qualitative research for education: An introduction to theory and methods.* Boston: Allyn and Bacon.

Bogdan, R., & Kugelmass, J. (1984). Case studies of mainstreaming: A symbolic interactionist approach to special schooling. In L. Barton & S. Tomlinson (Eds.), *Special education and social interests* (pp. 173–191). New York: Nichols Publishing.

Bogdan, R., & Taylor, S. J. (1976). The judged, not the judges: An insider's view of mental retardation. *American Psychologist, 31*(1), 47–52.

Bogdan, R., & Taylor, S. J. (1989). Relationships with severely disabled people: The social construction of humanness. *Social Problems, 36*(2), 135–148.

Bogdan, R., & Taylor, S. J. (1994). *The social meaning of mental retardation.* New York: Teachers College Press.

Booth, T. (1985). Labels and their consequences. In D. Lane & B. Stratford (Eds.), *Current approaches to Down's syndrome* (pp. 3–24). New York: Praeger.

Borthwick, C. (1996). Racism, IQ, and Down's syndrome. *Disability & Society, 11*(3), 403–410.

Botash, A. S., Babuts, D., Mitchell, N., O'Hara, M., Lynch, L., & Manuel, J. (1994). Evaluations of children who have disclosed sexual abuse via facilitated communication. *Archives of Pediatric and Adolescent Medicine, 148*, 1282–1287.

Bronston, W. (1995). Sandra Jensen's story. *Newsletter of the Association for Persons with Severe Handicaps, 21*(11/12), 18.

Brown, C. (1989). *My left foot.* New York: Simon & Schuster.

Brown, L. (1995). Inclusion in education and community life. In L. Nadel & D. Rosenthal (Eds.), *Living and learning in the community* (pp. 136–148). Baltimore: Brookes.

Buck, J. N. (1955). The sage: An unusual mongoloid. In A. Burton & R. Harris (Eds.), *Clinical studies of personality* (vol. 3; pp. 455–481). New York: Harper & Row.

Buck, P. S. (1950). *The child who never grew.* New York: John Day.

Buckley, S. (1985). Attaining basic educational skills: Reading, writing, and number. In D. Lane & B. Stratford (Eds.), *Current approaches to Down's syndrome* (pp. 315–344). New York: Praeger.

Buckley, S. (1995). Teaching children with Down syndrome to read and write. In L. Nadel & D. Rosenthal (Eds.), *Down syndrome: Living and learning in the community* (pp. 158–169). New York: Wiley-Liss.

Buckley, S., & Wood, E. (1983, December). *The extent and significance of reading skills in pre-school children with Down's syndrome.* Paper presented at the conference of the British Psychological Society, London.

Burke, C., & McDaniel, J. B. (1991). *A special kind of hero.* New York: Dell.

Butterfield, E. C. (1961). A provocative case of overachievement by a mongoloid. *American Journal on Mental Deficiency, 66*, 444–448.

Canning, C. D., & Pueschel, S. M. (1990). Developmental expectations: An overview. In S. M. Pueschel (Ed.), *A parent's guide to Down syndrome: Towards a brighter future* (pp. 93–102). Baltimore: Brookes.

Cardinal, D. N., Hanson, D., & Wakeham, J. (1996). Investigation of authorship in facilitated communication. *Mental Retardation, 34,* 231–242.

Case, R. D., Kurland, M., & Goldberg, J. (1982). Operational efficiency and the growth of short-term memory span. *Journal of Experimental Child Psychology, 33,* 386–404.

Chambers, R. (1890). *Vestiges of the natural history of creation.* London: Routledge. (Original work published 1844)

Cole, K. J., Abbs, J. H., & Turner, G. S. (1988). Deficits in the production of grip forces in Down syndrome. *Developmental Medicine and Child Neurology, 30,* 752–758.

Crookshank, F. G. (1931). *The mongol in our midst: A study of man and his three faces.* London: Kegan, Paul, Trench, Trubner.

Crossley, R. (1992, May). *Getting the words out.* Paper presented at the Facilitated Communication Institute Conference, Syracuse, NY.

Crossley, R. (1994). *Facilitated communication training.* New York: Teachers College Press.

Crossley, R., & McDonald, A. (1984). *Annie's coming out.* New York: Penguin.

Cunningham, P. M., & Allington, R. L. (1994). *Classrooms that work: They can all read and write.* New York: HarperCollins.

Darwin, C. (1963). *On the origin of species by the means of natural selection.* New York: Heritage Press. (Original work published 1859)

Dembo, M. H. (1988). *Applying educational psychology in the classroom* (3rd ed.) New York: Longman.

Descartes, R. (1951). *A discourse on method and selected writings* (J. Veitch, Trans.). New York: Dutton. (Original work published 1637)

Dewey, J. (1899). *School and society.* Chicago: University of Chicago Press.

Dewey, J. (1916). *Democracy and education: An introduction to the philosophy of education.* New York. MacMillan.

Dexter, L. A. (1994). On the politics and sociology of stupidity in our society. *Mental Retardation, 32,* 152–155. (Original work published 1964)

Dodd, B. (1975). Recognition and reproduction of words by Down syndrome and non–Down syndrome retarded children. *American Journal on Mental Deficiency, 80*(3), 306–311.

Down, J. L. (1866). Observations on an ethnic classification of idiots. *London Hospital Reports and Observations, 3,* 259–262.

Down, J. L. (1990). *Mental affiliations of childhood and youth.* London: MacKeith. (Original work published 1887)

Drake, S. (1993). Interactions of task demands, performance, and neurology. *Facilitated Communication Digest, 7*(4), 3–5.

Drew, C. J., Hardman, M. L., & Logan, D. R. (1996). *Mental retardation: A life cycle approach* (6th ed.). Englewood Cliffs, NJ: Merrill.

Duchan, J. F. (1993). Issues raised by facilitated communication for theorizing and research on autism. *Journal of Speech and Hearing Research, 36,* 1108–1119.

Dunn, L. M. (1968). Special education for the mildly retarded: Is much of it justifiable? *Exceptional Children, 35,* 5–22.

Durovich, C. (1990, February 9). Becky belongs. *Spartan Warrior, Winooski High School,* p. 2.

Dybwad, G. (1964). Are we retarding the retarded? In G. Dybwad (Ed.), *Challenges in mental retardation* (pp. 19–25). New York: Columbia University Press.

Dyson, A. H. (1993). *Social worlds of children learning to write in an urban primary school.* New York: Teachers College Press.

Eberlin, M., McConnachie, G., Ibel, S., & Volpe, L. (1993). Facilitated communication: A failure to replicate the phenomenon. *Journal of Autism and Developmental Disorders, 23,* 507–530.

Editors' Note. (1993). Film's description wrong. *Exceptional Parent, 23*(6), 6.

Elliott, D. (1985). Manual asymmetries in the performance of sequential movement by adolescents and adults with Down syndrome. *American Journal Of Mental Deficiency, 90*(1), 90–97.

Elliott, D., Gray, S., & Weeks, D. J. (1991). Verbal cuing and motor skills acquisition for adults with Down syndrome. *Adapted Physical Activity Quarterly, 8,* 210–220.

Falvey, M. A. (1995). *Inclusive and heterogeneous schooling: Assessment, curriculum, and instruction.* Baltimore: Brookes.

Falvey, M. A., Givner, C. C., & Kimm, C. (1996). What do I do Monday morning? In S. Stainback & W. Stainback (Eds.), *Inclusion: A guide for educators* (pp. 117–138). Baltimore: Brookes.

Feuerstein, R., Rand, Y., & Hoffman, M. B. (1979). *The dynamic assessment of retarded learners: The Learning Potential Assessment Device theory, instruments, and techniques.* Baltimore: University Park Press.

Feuerstein, R., Rand, Y., & Rynders, J. E. (1988). *Don't accept me as I am: Helping "retarded" people to excel.* New York: Plenum.

Fewell, R. R. (1991). Effective early intervention: Results from the model preschool program for children with Down syndrome and other developmental delays. *Topics in Early Childhood Special Education, 11*(1), 56–68.

Fishler, K., & Koch, R. (1991). Mental development in Down syndrome mosaicism. *American Journal On Mental Retardation, 96*(3), 345–351.

Florez, J. (1992). Neurological abnormalities. In S. M. Pueschel & J. K. Pueschel (Eds.), *Biomedical concerns in persons with Down syndrome* (pp. 159–173), Baltimore: Brookes.

Forness, S. R., & Knitzer, J. (1992). A new proposed definition and terminology to replace "serious emotional disturbance" in Individuals with Disabilities Act. *School Psychology Review, 21,* 12–20.

Foucault, M. (1965). *Madness and civilization: A history of insanity in the age of reason.* New York: Vintage.

Fowler, A. E., Doherty, B. J., & Boynton, L. (1995). Basis of reading skills in young adults with Down syndrome. In L. Nadel & D. Rosenthal (Eds.), *Down syndrome: Living and learning in the community* (pp. 182–196). New York: Wiley-Liss.

Fraser, J., & Mitchell, A. (1876). Kalmuc idiocy: Report of a case with autopsy and notes on 62 cases. *Journal of Mental Science, 22,* 161, 162, 169–179.

Freire, P. (1993). *Pedagogy of the oppressed* (rev. ed.). New York: Continuum.

Frith, U., & Frith, C. D. (1974). Specific motor disabilities in Down syndrome. *Journal of Child Psychology and Psychiatry, 15,* 283–301.

Fuller, P. R. (1949). Operant conditioning of a human vegetative organism. *American Journal of Psychology, 62*, 587–590.

Fulton, L., LeRoy, C., Pinckney, M., & Weekly, T. (1994). Peer education partners. *Teaching Exceptional Children, 26*, 6–11.

Furuno, S., O'Reilly, K. A., Hosaka, C. M., Inatsuka, T. T., Zeisloft-Falbey, B., & Allman, T. (1988). *Hawaii Early Learning Profile* (HELP). Palo Alto, CA: VORT.

Gardner, H. (1983). *Frames of mind: The theory of multiple intelligences.* New York: Basic Books.

Gardner, H. (1991). *The unschooled mind: How children think and how schools should teach.* New York: Basic Books.

Gardner, H. (1993). *Frames of mind: The theory of multiple intelligences* (rev. ed.). New York: Basic Books.

Gardner, H. (1995). Reflections on multiple intelligences: Myths and messages. *Phi Delta Kappan, 77*(4), 200–209.

Garton, A., & Pratt, C. (1989). *Learning to be literate: The development of written and spoken English.* Oxford: Blackwell.

Gelb, S. A. (1995). The beast in man: Degenerationism and mental retardation, 1900–1920. *Mental Retardation, 33*(1), 1–9.

Gibbs, E. D., Springer, A. S., Cooley, W. C., & Gray, S. (1993). *Early use of total communication: Parents' perspective on using sign language with young children with Down syndrome* (video). Baltimore: Brookes.

Gibson, D. (1978). *Down syndrome: The psychology of mongolism.* New York: Cambridge University Press.

Goddard, H. H. (1914). *Feeble-mindedness: Its causes and consequences.* New York: Macmillan.

Goffman, E. (1963). *Stigma: Notes on the management of spoiled identity.* Englewood Cliffs, NJ: Prentice-Hall.

Goldberg, C. (1996). Her survival proves doubters wrong: Sandra Jensen recovers from transplant she'd been denied. *Newsletter of the Association for Persons with Severe Handicaps, 22*(4), 21–22.

Goode, D. A. (1992). Who is Bobby?: Ideology and method in the discovery of a Down syndrome person's competence. In P. M. Ferguson, D. L. Ferguson, & S. J. Taylor (Eds.), *Interpreting disability: A qualitative reader* (pp. 197–212). New York: Teachers College Press.

Goodlad, J. (1983). A study of schooling: Some findings and hypotheses. *Phi Delta Kappan, 64*, 462–470.

Grandin, T., & Scariano, M. M. (1986). *Emergence: Labeled autistic.* Novato, CA: Arena.

Greeno, J. (1988). *Situations, mental models, and generative knowledge* (Tech. Rep. No. 5). Palo Alto, CA: Institute for Research in Learning.

Gwin, L. (1994, November/December). Who we are not. *New Mobility*, November/December, pp. 32–35.

Hallahan, D. P., & Kauffman, J. M. (1997). *Exceptional learners: Introduction to special education* (7th ed.). Boston: Allyn & Bacon.

Hamre-Nietupski, S., Hendrickson, J., Nietupski, J., & Shokoohi-Yekta, M. (1994). Regular educators' perceptions of facilitating friendships of students with moderate, severe, or profound disabilities with nondisabled peers. *Education and Training in Mental Retardation and Developmental Disabilities, 29*(2), 102–117.

Hansot, E. (1993). Historical and contemporary views of gender and education. In S. K. Biklen & D. Pollard (Eds.), *Gender and education* (pp. 12–24). Chicago: National Society for the Study of Education.

Harding, S. (1986). *The science question in feminism*. Ithaca, NY: Cornell University Press.

Hardman, M. L., Drew, C. J., & Egan, M. W. (1996). *Human exceptionality: Society, school, and family* (5th ed.). Boston: Allyn & Bacon.

Harris, T. (1994). Christine's inclusion: An example of peers supporting one another. In J. S. Thousand, R. A.Villa, & A. I. Nevin (Eds.), *Creativity and collaborative learning: A practical guide to empowering students* (pp. 293–304). Baltimore: Brookes.

Henderson, S. E., Illingsworth, S. M., & Allen, J. (1991). Prolongation of simple manual and vocal reaction times in Down syndrome. *Adapted Physical Activity Quarterly, 8*, 234–241.

Henderson, S. E., Morris, J., & Frith, U. (1981). The motor deficit in Down's syndrome children: A problem of timing? *Journal of Child Psychology and Psychiatry, 22*(3), 233–245.

Henderson, S. E., Morris, J., & Ray, S. (1981). Performance of Down syndrome and other retarded children on the Cratty Gross-Motor Test. *American Journal of Mental Deficiency, 85*(4), 416–424.

Heshusius, L. (1995). Holism and special education: There is no substitute for real life purposes and processes. In T. M. Skrtic (Ed.), *Disability and democracy: Reconstructing (special) education for postmodernity* (pp. 166–189). New York: Teachers College Press.

Heward, W. L. (1996). *Exceptional children: An introduction to special education* (5th ed.). Englewood Cliffs, NJ: Merrill.

Hodapp, R. M., & Zigler, E. (1990). Applying the developmental perspective to individuals with Down syndrome. In D. Cicchetti & M. Beeghly (Eds.), *Children with Down syndrome* (pp. 1–28). New York: Cambridge University Press.

Hollowood, T., Salisbury, C., Rainforth, D., & Palombaro, M. (1995). Use of instructional time in classrooms serving students with and without severe disabilities. *Exceptional Children, 61*(3), 242–253.

Hubert, C. (1997, May 25). Transplant pioneer loses battle for life. *The Sacramento (Califronia) Bee*, p. A1.

Hudson, A., Melita, B., & Arnold, N. (1993). Brief report: A case study assessing the validity of facilitated communication. *Journal of Autism and Developmental Disorders, 23*, 165–173.

Hunt, N. (1966). *The world of Nigel Hunt: The diary of a mongoloid youth*. New York: Garrett.

Hunt, N., & Marshall, K. (1994). *Exceptional children and youth*. Geneva, IL: Houghton Mifflin.

Hunt, P., Staub, D., Alwell, M., & Goetz, L. (1994). Achievements by all students within the context of cooperative learning groups. *The Journal of the Association for Persons with Severe Handicaps, 19*(4), 290–301.

IDRP (Intellectual Disability Review Panel). (1989). *Investigation into the reliability and validity of the assisted communication technique*. Victoria, Australia: Department of Community Services.

Illingsworth, R. S. (1974). *The child at school*. Oxford: Blackwell.

Ireland, W. (1877). *On idiocy and imbecility*. London: J. & A. Churchill.

Irwin, K. C. (1991). Teaching children with Down syndrome to add by counting on. *Education and Treatment of Children, 14*(2), 128–141.

Jago, J. L., Jago, A. G., & Hart, M. (1984). An evaluation of the total communication approach for teaching language skills to developmentally delayed preschool children. *Education and training of the mentally retarded, 19*(3), 175–182.

Janzen-Wilde, M. L., Duchan, J. F., & Higgenbotham, D. J. (1995). Successful use of facilitated communication with an oral child. *Journal of Speech and Hearing Research, 38*, 658–676.

Jensen, S. (1996, November). *Inspiration, self-determination, and controlling your own destiny*. Keynote address at the annual conference of the Association for Persons with Severe Handicaps, New Orleans.

Johnson-Martin, N., Attermeier, S., & Hacker, B. (1990). *Carolina curriculum for preschoolers with special needs*. Baltimore, MD: Brookes.

Jungck, S., & Marshall, J. D. (1992). Curricular perspectives on one great debate. In S. Kessler & B. B. Swadener (Eds.), *Reconceptualizing the early childhood curriculum: Beginning the dialogue* (pp. 93–102). New York: Teachers College Press.

Kamps, D. M., Leonard, B., Potucek, J., & Garrison-Harrell, L. (1995). Cooperative learning groups in reading: An integration strategy for students with autism and general classroom peers. *Behavioral Disorders, 21*(1), 89–109.

Kangas, K., & Lloyd, L. (1988). Early cognitive skills as prerequisites to augmentative and alternative communication: What are we waiting for? *Alternative and Augmentative Communication, 4*, 211–221.

Kanner, L. (1942). Exoneration of the feebleminded. *American Journal of Psychiatry, 99*, 17–22.

Kanner, L. (1964). *A history of the care and study of the mentally retarded*. Springfield, IL: Thomas.

Kauffman, J. M. (1995, April). *Why we must celebrate a diversity of restrictive environments*. Keynote address at the annual convention of the Council for Exceptional Children, Indianapolis, IN.

Kaufman, A. S., & Kaufman, N. L. (1984). *Kaufman Assessment Battery for Children*. Circle Pines, MN: American Guidance Service.

Kazdin, A. E. (1989). *Behavior modification in applied settings* (4th ed.). Pacific Grove, CA: Brookes/Cole.

Kennedy, F. (1942). The problem of social control of the congenital defective: Education, sterilization, euthanasia. *American Journal of Psychiatry, 99*, 13–16.

Kerr, J. (1926). *The fundamentals of school health*. London: George Allen & Unwin.

Kingsley, E. P., & Levitz, B. G. (1994). Introduction. In J. Kingsley & M. Levitz, *Count us in: Growing up with Down syndrome* (pp. 1–9). San Diego: Harcourt Brace.

Kingsley, J. (1996). Developmental disabilities. *D.S. Headline News, 2*(2), 6.

Kingsley, J., & Levitz, M. (1994). *Count us in: Growing up with Down syndrome*. San Diego: Harcourt Brace.

Kliewer, C., & Biklen, D. (1996). Labelling: Who wants to be called retarded? In W. Stainback & S. Stainback (Eds.), *Controversial issues confronting special education: Divergent perspectives* (2nd ed., pp. 83–95). Boston: Allyn & Bacon.

Kliewer, C., & Drake, S. (1998). Disability, eugenics, and the current ideology of segregation: A modern moral tale. *Disability & Society, 13*(1).

Knoblock, P. (1978). An alternative learning environment: Its impact on prevention. In S. J. Apter (Ed.), *Focus on prevention* (pp. 21–40). Syracuse, NY: Syracuse University Press.

Knoblock, P. (Ed.). (1982). *Teaching and mainstreaming autistic children*. Denver: Love.

Koppenhaver, D. A., Pierce, P. L., & Yoder, D. E. (1995). AAC, FC, and the ABCs: Issues and relationships. *American Journal of Speech-Language Pathology, 4*, 5–14.

Kouri, T. (1989). How manual sign acquisition relates to the development of spoken language: A case study. *Language. Speech, and Hearing Services In Schools, 20*, 50–62.

Kozol, J. (1991). *Savage inequalities: Children in America's schools*. New York: HarperCollins.

Kumin, L. (1994). *Communication skills in children with Down syndrome: A guide for parents*. Rockville, MD: Woodbine House.

Kunc, N. (1993, May). *Beyond benevolence*. Keynote address at the annual conference of the Facilitated Communication Institute, Syracuse, NY.

Lane, D., & Stratford, B. (Eds.). (1985). *Current approaches to Down's syndrome*. New York: Praeger.

Lane, D., & Stratford, B. (Eds.). (1987). *Current approaches to Down's syndrome* (2nd ed.). New York: Praeger.

Lane, H. (1979). *The wild boy of Aveyron*. Cambridge, MA: Harvard University Press.

LeClair, D. A., Pollock, B. J., & Elliott, D. (1993). Movement preparation in adults with and without Down syndrome. *American Journal on Mental Retardation, 97*(6), 628–633.

Lejeune, J., Gautier, M., & Turpin, R. (1959). Études des chromosomes somatiques de neuf enfants mongoliens. *Comptes Rendus l'Academie des Sciences, 248*, 1721.

Lewis, R. (1997). *Human genetics: Concepts and applications* (2nd ed.). Dubuque, IA: Brown.

Lieberman, L. M. (1996). Preserving special education . . . for those who need it. In W. Stainback & S. Stainback (Eds.), *Controversial issues confronting special education: Divergent perspectives* (2nd ed; pp. 16–27). Boston: Allyn & Bacon.

Lipsky, D. K., & Gartner, A. (Eds.). (1989). *Beyond separate education: Quality education for all*. Baltimore: Brookes.

Logan, K. R., Diaz, E., Piperno, M., Rankin, D., MacFarland, A. D., & Bargamian, K. (1994/1995). How inclusion built a community of learners. *Educational Leadership, 52*(4), 42–45.

Luke, M. (1995). A demonstration of "natural supports" on the international scene: Bad grades—solidarity action. *Down Syndrome News, 18*(3), 30.

Luther, M. (1959). Colloquia mensalia. In *What Luther says* (Vol. 3). St. Louis, MO: Concordia. (Original work published 1652)

MacMillan, D. L. (1982). *Mental retardation in school and society* (2nd ed.). Boston: Little, Brown.

MacPherson, C. B. (1974). *The life and times of liberal democracy*. Oxford: Oxford University Press.

McGee, J. J., Menolascino, F. J., Hobbs, D. C., & Menousek, P. E. (1987). *Gentle teaching: A non-aversive approach to helping persons with mental retardation*. New York: Human Sciences Press.

McKay, J. P., Hill, B. D., & Buckler, J. (1983). *The history of Western society* (2nd ed.). Boston: Houghton Mifflin.

Mercer, J. (1973). *Labeling the mentally retarded: Clinical and social system perspectives on mental retardation*. Berkeley: University of California Press.

Merton, T. A. (1968). *Mankind in the unmaking: The anthropology of mongolism*. Melbourne: Fairlight.

Meyers, L. F. (1986). Teaching language. *Exceptional Parent, 16*(7), 20–23.

Meyers, L. F. (1988). Using computers to teach children with Down's syndrome spoken and written language skills. In L. Nadel (Ed.), *The psychobiology of Down's syndrome* (pp. 247–265). New York: National Down Syndrome Society.

Meyers, L. F. (1990). Language development and intervention. In D. C. Van Dyke, D. J. Lang, F. Heide, S. van Duyne, & M. J. Soucek (Eds.), *Clinical perspectives in the management of Down's syndrome* (pp. 153–164). New York: Springer-Verlag.

Miller, J. F. (1987). Language and communication characteristics of children with Down syndrome. In S. M. Pueschel, C. Tingey, J. E. Rynders, A. C. Crocker, & D. M. Crutcher (Eds.), *New perspectives on Down syndrome* (pp. 233–262). Baltimore: Brookes.

Mills v. D.C. Board of Education, 348 F. Supp. 866 (D.D.C. 1972).

Montessori, M. (1967). *The absorbent mind* (C.A. Claremont, trans.). New York: Holt, Rinehart & Winston. (Original work published 1949)

Moon, E. (1992). Test child/real child. *Exceptional Parent, 22*(4), 16–19.

Moore, S., Donovan, B., & Hudson, A. (1993). Facilitator suggested conversational evaluation of facilitated communication. *Journal of Autism and Developmental Disorders, 23*, 541–551.

Murphy, T. J. (1994). Handicapping education. *National Review, 46*(17), 56–58.

Nadel, L., & Rosenthal, D. (Eds.). (1995). *Down syndrome: Living and learning in the community*. New York: Wiley-Liss.

Nehring, A. D., Nehring, E. F., Bruni, J. R., & Randolph, P. L. (1992). *Learning Accomplishments Profile–Diagnostic Standardized Assessment*. Lewisville, NC: Kaplan School Supply Corporation.

Nolan, C. (1987). *Under the eye of the clock*. New York: St. Martin's Press.

Oberti v. Board of Education of the Borough of Clementon School District et al., 789 F. Supp. 1322 (D. NJ 1992).

Oberti v. Board of Education of the Borough of Clementon School District et al., 995 F.2nd 1204 (3d Cir. 1993).

O'Donnell, M. P., & Wood, M, (1992). *Becoming a reader: A developmental approach to reading*. Boston: Allyn & Bacon.

Oelwein, P. L. (1995). *Teaching reading to children with Down syndrome: A guide for parents and teachers*. Rockville, MD: Woodbine House.

Ohr, P. S., & Fagen, J. W. (1991). Conditioning and long-term memory in three-month-old infants with Down syndrome. *American Journal on Mental Retardation, 96*(2), 151–162.

Olney, M. (1995). *A controlled evaluation of facilitated communication*. Unpublished doctoral dissertation, Syracuse University, Syracuse, NY.

Oppenheim, R. C. (1977). *Effective teaching methods for autistic children*. Springfield, IL: Charles C. Thomas.

P. F. (1993). Film's description wrong. *Exceptional Parent, 23*(6), 6.

Patton, J. M., & Payne, J. S. (1989). Mild mental retardation. In N. G. Haring (Ed.), *Exceptional children and youth* (3rd ed; pp. 112–130). Columbus, OH: Merrill.

Pecyna, P. M. (1988). Rebus symbol communication training with a severely handicapped preschool child: A case study. *Language, Speech, and Hearing Services In Schools, 19*, 128–143.

Pennsylvania Association for Retarded Children v. Commonwealth of Pennsylvania, 343 F. Supp. 279 (E.D. Penn. 1972).

Penrose, L. S. (1966). Foreword. In N. Hunt, *The world of Nigel Hunt: The diary of a mongoloid youth* (pp. 9–13). New York: Garrett.

Perske, R. (1987). Attitudes, acceptance, and awareness: The changing view towards persons with Down's syndrome. In S. M. Pueschel, C. Tingey, J. E. Rynders, A. C. Crocker, & D. M. Crutcher (Eds.), *New perspectives in Down syndrome* (pp. 273–288). Baltimore: Brookes.

Peterson, M. (1994). Taking charge of my education. *D.S. Headline News, 1*(1), 6–7.

Peterson, M. (1996). Doing research on how we learn language. *D.S. Headline News, 2*(1), 5.

Pick, D. (1989). *Faces of degeneration: A European disorder, 1848–1918*. Cambridge, U.K.: Cambridge University Press.

Pieterse, M., & Treloar, R. (1981). *The Down's syndrome program* (Progress report 1981). London: MacQuarie University.

Poplin, M. (1988). Holistic/constructivist principles of the teaching/learning process: Implications for the field of learning disabilities. *Journal of Learning Disabilities, 21*(7), 401–416.

Poplin, M., Wiest, D. J., & Thorson, S. (1996). Alternative instructional strategies to reductionism: Constructive, critical, multicultural, and feminine pedagogies. In W. Stainback & S. Stainback (Eds.), *Controversial issues confronting special education: Divergent perspectives* (2nd ed.; pp. 153–165). Boston: Allyn & Bacon.

Pototzky, C., & Grigg, A. E. (1942). A revision of the prognosis in mongolism. *American Journal of Orthopsychiatry, 12*(3), 503–510.

Pugach, M. C., & Wesson, C. L. (1995). Teachers' and students' views of team teaching of general education and learning disabled students in two 5th grade classes. *The Elementary School Journal, 95*, 279–296.

Resnick, D. P., & Resnick, L. B. (1977). The nature of literacy: An historical exploration. *Harvard Educational Review, 47*(3), 370–385.

Restak, R. (1975). Genetic counseling for defective parents: The danger of knowing too much. *Psychology Today, 9*, 21–23, 92–93.

Rhodes, W. C. (1995). Liberatory pedagogy and special education. *Journal of Learning Disabilities, 28*(8), 458–462.

Roch, R. (1978). Gestural facilitation of expressive language in moderately/severely retarded preschoolers. *Mental Retardation, 16,* 113–117.

Rogers, D. E. (1953). *Angel unaware.* Westwood, NJ: Revell.

Rosenzweig, L. E. (1953). School training of the mongoloid child. In *Mongolism: A symposium* (pp. 281–289). New York: Jewish Hospital of Brooklyn.

Rothman, D. J., & Rothman, S. M. (1984). *The Willowbrook wars.* New York: Harper & Row.

Ruhräh, J. (1935). Cretin or Mongol, or both together? *American Journal of Disabled Children, 49,* 477–478.

Ryndak, D. L., & Alper, S. (1996). *Curriculum content for students with severe disabilities in inclusive settings.* Boston: Allyn & Bacon.

Rynders, J. E. (1987). The history of Down syndrome: The need for a new perspective. In S. M. Pueschel, C. Tingey, J. E. Rynders, A. C. Crocker & D. M. Crutcher (Eds.), *New perspectives in Down syndrome* (pp. 1–20). Baltimore: Brookes.

Rynders, J. E., & Horrobin, J. (1975). Project EDGE: A communication stimulation program for Down's syndrome infants. In B. Friedlander, G. Sterritt, & G. Kirk (Eds.), *Exceptional infant: Assessment and intervention* (vol. 3; pp. 173–192). New York: Bruner/Mazel.

Rynders, J. E., & Horrobin, J. (1980). Educational provisions for young children with Down's syndrome. In J. Gottlieb (Ed.), *Educating mentally retarded persons in the mainstream* (pp. 109–147). Baltimore: University Park Press.

Rynders, J. E., & Horrobin, J. (1990). Always trainable? Never educable? Updating educational expectations concerning children with Down syndrome. *American Journal on Mental Retardation, 95*(1), 77–83.

Rynders, J. E., Spiker, D., & Horrobin, J. M. (1978). Underestimating the educability of Down syndrome children: Examination of methodological problems in recent literature. *American Journal of Mental Deficiency, 82,* 440–448.

Sapon-Shevin, M., Ayres, B. J., & Duncan, J. (1994). Cooperative learning and inclusion. In J. S. Thousand, R. A. Villa, & A. I. Nevin (Eds.), *Creativity and collaborative learning: A practical guide to empowering students and teachers* (pp. 45–58). Baltimore: Brookes.

Sarason, S. B. (1959). *Psychological problems in mental deficiency* (3rd ed.). New York: Harper.

Sarason, S. B., Davidson, K., & Blatt, B. (1962). *The preparation of teachers: An unstudied problem in education.* New York: Wiley.

Sarason, S. B. & Doris, J. (1969). *Psychological problems in mental deficiency* (4th ed.) New York: Harper & Row.

Sarason, S. B., & Doris, J. (1979). *Educational handicap, public policy, and social history: A broadened perspective on mental retardation.* New York: Free Press.

Scheerenberger, R. C. (1983). *A history of mental retardation.* Baltimore: Brookes.

Schein, E. H. (1972). *Professional education: Some new directions.* New York: McGraw-Hill.

Schnorr, R. F. (1990). "Peter? He comes and goes . . .": First graders' perspectives on a part-time mainstream student. *Journal Of the Association for Persons with Severe Handicaps, 15*(4), 231–240.

Schön, D. A. (1983). *The reflective practitioner: How professionals think in action.* New York: Basic Books.

Schopler, E., Mesibov, G. B., & Hearsey, K. (1995). Structured teaching in the TEACCH system. In E. Schopler & G. B. Mesibov (Eds.), *Learning and cognition in autism* (pp. 243–268). New York: Plenum.

Seagoe, M. V. (1964). *Yesterday was Tuesday, all day and all night: The story of a unique education.* Boston: Little, Brown.

Seguin, E. (1907). *Idiocy: And its treatment by the physiological method.* New York: Teachers College. (Original work published 1866)

Sendak, M. (1961). *Where the wild things are.* New York: Harper & Row.

Sendak, M. (1970). *In the night's kitchen.* New York: Harper & Row.

Serafica, F. C. (1990). Peer relations of children with Down syndrome. In D. Cicchetti & M. Beeghly (Eds.), *Children with Down syndrome: A developmental perspective* (pp. 369–398). New York: Cambridge University Press.

Shannon, P. (1990). *The struggle to continue: Progressive reading instruction in the United States.* Portsmouth, NH: Heinemann.

Shapiro, J. P. (1994). *No pity: People with disabilities forging a new civil rights movement.* New York: Times Books.

Shapiro, J. P., Loeb, P., Bowermaster, D., & Toch, T. (1993, December 13). Separate and unequal: How special education programs are cheating our children and costing taxpayers billions each year. *U.S. News & World Report, 115*(23), 46–60.

Sheehan, C., & Matuozzi, R. (1996). Validation of facilitated communication, *Mental Retardation, 34,* 94–107.

Shevin, M. (1993). Who are our Phillis Wheatleys? *Facilitated Communication Digest, 1*(3), 1–2.

Simon, E. W., Toll, D. M., & Whitehair, P. M. (1994). A naturalistic approach to the validation of facilitated communication. *Journal of Autism and Developmental Disorders, 24,* 647–657.

Simons-Derr, J. A. (1983). Signing vs. silence. *The Exceptional Parent, 13*(6), 49–52.

Simpson, R. L., & Myles, B. S. (1995). Effectiveness of facilitated communication with children and youth with autism. *Journal of Special Education, 28,* 424–439.

Singham, M. (1995). Race and intelligence: What are the issues? *Phi Delta Kappan, 77*(4), 271–278.

Sinson, J. C., & Wetherick, N. E. (1981). The behaviour of children with Down's syndrome in normal playgroups. *Journal of Mental Deficiency Research, 25*(2), 113–120.

Skrtic, T. M. (Ed.). (1995a). *Disability and democracy: Reconstructing (special) education for postmodernity* (pp. 65–103). New York: Teachers College Press.

Skrtic, T. M. (1995b). The functionalist view of special education and disability: Deconstructing the conventional knowledge tradition. In T. M. Skrtic (Ed.), *Disability and democracy: Reconstructing (special) education for postmodernity* (pp. 65–103). New York: Teachers College Press.

Sleeter, C. E. (1986). Learning disabilities: The social construction of a special education category. *Exceptional Children, 53*(1), 46–54.

Smith, F. (1988a). *Joining the literacy club.* Portsmouth, NH: Heinemann.

Smith, F. (1988b). *Understanding reading* (4th ed.). Hillsdale, NJ: Erlbaum.

Smith, J. D. (1985). *Minds made feeble: The myth and legacy of the Kallikaks.* Austin, TX: Pro-Ed.

Snow, J. (1988). Bradwyn Address, 89th annual meeting of Frontier College, Toronto, Ontario. (Reprinted in M. Forest & B. Kappel (Eds.), *It's about learning* (pp. 143–149). Toronto: Frontier College Press.)

Snow, J. A. (1996). Responding to the death of Tracy Latimer. In J. Pearpoint & M. Forest (Eds.), *Inclusion News 1996* (p. 12). Toronto: Inclusion Press International.

Sobsey, D., & Dreimanis, M. (1993). Integration outcomes: Theoretical models and empirical investigations. *Developmental Disabilities Bulletin, 21,* 1–15.

Solsken, J. W. (1993). *Literacy, gender, and work: In families and in schools.* Norwood, NJ: Ablex.

Soltis, J. F. (1993). Democracy and teaching. *Journal of Philosophy of Education, 27*(2), 149–158.

Spock, B. (1949). *The pocket book of baby and child care.* New York: Pocket Books.

Stainback, S., & Stainback, W. (Eds.). (1996). *Inclusion: A guide for educators.* Baltimore: Brookes.

Stanton, J. (1997, July 3). District to go to early dismissal. *The Waterloo/Cedar Falls (Iowa) Journal Courier,* p. B1.

Staub, D., & Peck, C. A. (1994/1995). What are the outcomes for nondisabled students? *Educational Leadership, 52*(4), 36–41.

Steering Committee. (1993). *The Queensland report on facilitated communication.* Queensland, Australia: Department of Family Services and Aboriginal and Islander Affairs, Division of Intellectual Disability Services.

Still, G. F. (1909). *Common disorders and diseases of childhood.* London: Hodder & Stoughton.

Stratford, B., & Metcalfe, A. (1982). Recognition, reproduction, and recall in children with Down's syndrome. *Australian and New Zealand Journal of Developmental Disabilities, 8,* 125–132.

Szempruch, J., & Jacobson, J. W. (1993). Evaluating the facilitated communications of people with developmental disabilities. *Research in Developmental Disabilities, 14,* 253–264.

Taylor, S. J. (1988). Caught in the continuum: A critical analysis of the least restrictive environment. *Journal of the Association for Persons with Severe Handicaps, 13*(1), 41–53.

Taylor, S. J., & Searl, S. J. (1987). The disabled in America: History, policy, and trends. In P. Knoblock (Ed.), *Understanding exceptional children and youth* (pp. 5–64). Boston: Little, Brown.

Thomas, G. E. (1996). *Teaching students with mental retardation: A life goal curriculum planning approach.* Englewood Cliffs, NJ: Merrill.

Thousand, J. S., & Villa, R. A. (1995). Managing complex change toward inclusive schooling. In R. A. Villa & J. S. Thousand (Eds.). *Creating an inclusive school* (pp. 51–79). Alexandria, VA: Association for Supervision and Curriculum Development.

Tingey, C. (1988). *Down syndrome: A resource handbook.* Boston: College-Hill.

Tredgold, A. F. (1929). *Mental deficiency* (5th ed.). London: Bailliere, Tindall, & Cox.

Trent, J. W., Jr. (1994). *Inventing the feeble mind: A history of mental retardation in the United States.* Berkeley: University of California Press.

Tzuriel, D. (1992). The dynamic assessment approach: A reply to Frisby and Braden. *The Journal of Special Education, 26*(3), 302–324.

Udvari-Solner, A. (1995). A process for adapting curriculum in inclusive classrooms. In Villa, R. A., & Thousand, J. S. (Eds.), *Creating an inclusive school* (pp. 110–124). Alexandria, VA: Association for Supervision and Curriculum Development.

Van der Klift, E., & Kunc, N. (1994). Friendship and the politics of help. In J. S. Thousand, R. A.Villa, & A. I. Nevin (Eds.), *Creativity and collaborative learning: A practical guide to empowering students* (pp. 391–401). Baltimore: Brookes.

Vargo, R., & Vargo, J. (1995). Voice of inclusion: My friend, Ro Vargo. In R. A. Villa & J. S. Thousand (Eds.), *Creating an inclusive school* (pp. 45–50). Alexandria, VA: Association for Supervision and Curriculum Development.

Villa, R. A., & Thousand, J. S. (Eds.). (1995). *Creating an inclusive school.* Alexandria, VA: Association for Supervision and Curriculum Development.

Villa, R. A., Udis, J., & Thousand, J. S. (1994). Responses for children experiencing behavioral and emotional challenges. In J. S. Thousand, R. A. Villa, & A. I. Nevin (Eds.), *Creativity and collaborative learning: A practical guide to empowering students* (pp. 369–390). Baltimore: Brookes.

Volpe, E. P. (1986). Is Down syndrome a modern disease? *Perspectives in Biology and Medicine, 29*(3), 423–436.

Vygotsky, L. S. (1978). *Mind in society: The development of higher mental processes* (M. Cole, V. John-Steiner, S. Scribner, & E. Souberman, Trans.). Cambridge, MA: Harvard University Press. (Original works published 1930–1935)

Vygotsky, L. S. (1981). The genesis of higher mental functions. In J. V. Wertsch (Ed.), *The concept of activity in Soviet psychology* (pp. 144–188). Armonk, NY: Sharpe.

Vygotsky, L. S. (1993). *The collected works of L. S. Vygotsky: The fundamentals of defectology* (vol. 2; R. W. Rieber & A. S. Carton, Eds.; J. E. Knox & C. B. Stevens, Trans.). New York: Plenum.

Walkerdine, V. (1990). *Schoolgirl fictions.* New York: Verso.

Weiler, K. (1988). *Women teaching for change: Gender, class, and power.* New York: Bergin & Garvey.

Weingold, J. T. (1953). Rehabilitation of the mongoloid child. In *Mongolism: A symposium* (pp. 253–254). New York: Jewish Hospital of Brooklyn.

Weiss, M. J. S., Wagner, S. H., & Bauman, M. L. (1996). A validated case study of facilitated communication. *Mental Retardation, 4,* 220–230.

What's Happening. (1993). Documentary about learning disability wins academy award. *Exceptional Parent, 23*(4), 50.

Wheeler, D. L., Jacobson, J. W., Paglieri, R. A., & Schwartz, A. A. (1993). An ex-
    perimental assessment of facilitated communication. *Mental Retardation*, *31*(1),
    49–60.
Wilson, M. (1997, January 31). Grit won her a new heart: Disabled woman doing
    well a year after transplant. *San Francisco Chronicle*, p. A19.
Winship, A. E. (1900). *Jukes—Edwards: A study in education and heredity*. Harris-
    burg, PA: Myers.
Wolf, J. M., & McAlonic, M. L. (1977). A multimodality language program for re-
    tarded preschoolers. *Education and Training for the Mentally Retarded*, *12*,
    197–202.

Index

About the Author

Christopher Kliewer is an assistant professor in the Department of Special Education at the University of Northern Iowa in Cedar Falls, where he teaches undergraduate courses on issues in inclusive schooling, and is involved in family advocacy work. Earlier, he taught in self-contained schools for students with disabilities and in inclusive classrooms. His teaching experiences led him to complete a Ph.D. in Teaching and Leadership at Syracuse University in 1995. His studies have focused on critical issues involved in the ending of segregated schooling, literacy acquisition in young children, communication development in students with disabilities, and qualitative methods in educational inquiry. His publications have appeared in a number of journals, including *Mental Retardation*, *Exceptional Children*, *Disability & Society*, and the *Journal of the Association for Persons with Severe Disabilities*.